FALLING
IN LOVE
═══ WITH ═══
GOD

FALLING
IN LOVE
—— WITH ——
GOD

BOB HOSTETLER

LEAFWOOD
PUBLISHERS

FALLING IN LOVE WITH GOD
Copyright 2013 by Bob Hostetler

ISBN 978-0-89112-374-3
LCCN 2012037070

Printed in the United States of America

Published in association with The Steve Laube Agency, 5025 N. Central Ave., #635, Phoenix, AZ 85012.

LIBRARY OF CONGRESS CATALOGING-IN-PUBLICATION DATA
Hostetler, Bob, 1958-
 Falling in love with God / by Bob Hostetler.
    pages ; cm
 ISBN 978-0-89112-374-3
 1. God (Christianity)--Worship and love. 2. Spiritual life--Christianity. 3. Bible. O.T. Hosea--Criticism, interpretation, etc. I. Title.
 BV4817.H67 2013
 248.4--dc23

                                                                    2012037070

Cover design by Marc Whitaker | Interior text design by Sandy Armstrong

Leafwood Publishers is an imprint of Abilene Christian University Press
1626 Campus Court | Abilene, Texas 79601
1-877-816-4455 | www.leafwoodpublishers.com

13 14 15 16 17 18 / 7 6 5 4 3 2 1

Dedicated to

Aubrey and Kevin
Aaron and Nina

Table of Contents

Acknowledgments

Thank you to my agent and friend, Steve Laube of the Steve Laube Agency, for representing me on this project.

Thank you to Dr. Leonard Allen, Gary Myers, Robyn Burwell, and all the folks at Leafwood Publishers for believing in this book and its message, for their vision and flexibility, and for the inestimable expertise that made it better at every point in the process.

Thank you to the prayer team who faithfully prayed for me and for this project: Julie Webb, Doug Webb, Julie Sellers, Scott Sellers, Suzan Hughes, Dewey Hughes, Denise Antonius, and Gary Antonius. Your ministry to me and to the readers of this book is immeasurable.

Thank you also—as always—to the lovely Robin, my wife. You are and always have been a best friend, boon companion, confidante, lover, teacher, conscience, supporter, encourager, and muse to me.

Author's Note

If you were asked to list the greatest love songs of all time, what songs would come to mind first? The Righteous Brothers' "Unchained Melody?" Percy Sledge's "When a Man Loves a Woman?" "Some Enchanted Evening," from the Rodgers and Hammerstein musical *South Pacific*? Something by Barry White? Whitney Houston? Adele?

Mine would all be sentimental choices: Joe Cocker's rendition of "You Are So Beautiful." Paul McCartney's "Maybe I'm Amazed." And Nat King Cole's "That Sunday, That Summer." Oh, and Hosea. By Hosea.

I know, that last one may seem strange. But I honestly think the book of Hosea, tucked away in the last hundred pages or so of the Old Testament in the Bible, is a love song for today. It's never been a Top Ten hit. In fact, you may never have read the whole thing. But I hope by the end of this book you'll agree with me: it is a love song for the ages, one that can actually kindle love in the human heart.

There are a few things I'd like to explain about this book. First, I've taken the unusual liberty of using my own personal paraphrase of Hosea as the primary text throughout this book. This is not because I am a translator or scholar; I am neither. I am, however, a reader and lover of God's Word, the Bible. So, my paraphrase of Hosea's fourteen chapters is written from that perspective and no other. In it, I tried to convey as smoothly and powerfully as possible the love of God that seems to me to virtually ooze from every line. Throughout, I also tried to reduce confusion for the modern reader as much as possible. So, for example, while the nation of Israel is sometimes called Israel, sometimes Jacob, and sometimes Ephraim in the original text (and most translations), I stuck with Israel. I also did my best to convey the general thought or sentiment of a verse or passage, while often summarizing or condensing some parts. However, I want to make it clear that I do not intend or imagine my paraphrase to be in any way preferable or superior to the many excellent translations that are available; I strongly urge the reader to consult those versions for study and further reading and allow any mistakes or misjudgments on my part to be corrected by them.

Also, in the chapters that follow, I've chosen song titles as subheads. In so doing, I do not mean to endorse any of the songs, songwriters, or performing artists who are associated with the song but intend them only as a way of emphasizing the romance of the book's message.

Finally, I have ended Chapters Three through Eleven with prayers, to help you personalize and internalize the content of the preceding chapter. I hope you won't skip the prayer. In fact, I hope you won't simply read it, as simply intellectually absorbing the content won't change much, if anything. I hope you will take the time and thought to actually pray it. I believe that is a key part of the process. Sincerely praying these prayers will make you a partner with the Holy Spirit in bringing about not just "head improvement" but "heart movement," which is the purpose for which I write.

Bob Hostetler
February 2013

_1_

Why Fall
in Love?

*N*ot long ago, a friend of mine told me the story of an evening
when he, his wife, and a few friends from church were sit-
ting in his home, talking about the life of faith. In the course of the
conversation, someone used the phrase "falling in love with God."
A few moments later, someone else said something similar, and still
another added a mention of being "in love" with God.

The conversation broadened and deepened over the next few
moments until Melissa, a young mother in the group who usually
listened and smiled without saying much, finally summoned all
her courage.

"What are you guys talking about?" she asked. "What do you
mean, 'fall in love with God'?"

The room fell silent.

A few of them looked around at each other. Some stared at the
ceiling. Or the floor.

But no one had an answer.

Believe it or not, that's not unusual.

Some people talk about falling in love with God. And some people—perhaps the majority—have no idea what they're talking about. It's not uncommon for me to talk about being in love with God and see the head of the person I'm talking to tilt to one side, like that of a robin listening for the first worm of spring. Sometimes my listeners will let me keep talking, but occasionally they'll stop me to ask, "What are you talking about?" And some are even so bold as to press me for information, asking, "How's that work? How does a person fall in love with God?"

How *does* that work? How *does* a person fall in love with God? For some people, it seemed to just happen; they never had to think much about it. But others can't imagine what kind of person would speak in those terms or what kind of experience that would be. Is it a mystical kind of thing? Is it reserved only for the superspiritual? Or the lunatic fringe? Or can anyone do it? And why would anyone want to?

That's what this book is about.

Why Do Fools Fall in Love?

It was a fragrant June day when I first asked the lovely Robin Wright to go out with me. I was fifteen. She was fifteen. We were both on the staff of a Christian camp near Cincinnati, Ohio. She was far and away the loveliest creature I had ever seen: tall, tanned, lithe, with brown hair that cascaded to her waist. I threw caution to the wind and asked her out. She politely turned me down, explaining that someone else had already asked her.

She dated that "someone else" for the rest of the summer. The next summer, I played it cool. I didn't ask her out. But I also barely let her out of my sight. After a few evenings of "hanging out" together, she pointed out that while we were spending large chunks of time with each other, I had never officially asked her out. So I did. And—amazingly, mercifully, wonderfully—she said yes.

I don't know how long it took. I don't know just when it happened. But at some point, my teenage infatuation (and hormonal impulses) turned undeniably into love. At some point, I told her I loved her and she said she loved me, too. After dating for two years, I asked her to marry me, and she said yes. Three years after our first date (when we were both incredibly mature nineteen-year-olds), we became husband and wife.

Why did I fall in love? Because she was beautiful, of course. And charming. And intelligent. And fun, kind, virtuous, and interesting. But there was more to it than that. I wanted to fall in love. I wanted her to fall in love with me. I wanted us to be in love together.

But again—why? Why did I *want* to fall in love? Why does *anyone* want to fall in love?

Some might say we fall in love because we are biologically driven to reproduce ourselves, to propagate the human species. Others might suggest we fall in love because we seek "self-actualization," the fulfillment of our maximum potential. Could be. But I think the answer is a lot simpler than either of those reasons.

I think we want to fall in love because we instinctively sense—or perhaps know—that love is the most pleasurable of all human sensations. Love makes us feel good. Love makes us happy. Love satisfies our deepest needs. As the pop standard "Nature Boy" says, "The greatest thing you'll ever learn is just to love, and be loved in return."[1]

That has been my experience, not only in my relationship with my wife but also in my relationship with God. I want to fall in love with God, at least partly, for the same reason I wanted to fall in love with Robin—it is fulfilling. It is pleasurable. It rocks me like a hurricane. And it's not just me. It does the same for anyone.

It will do the same for you.

Love Can Make You Happy

When God got things started on this little blue ball we call Earth, he built love into his creation. Among the countless sources of joy and fulfillment God installed in the Garden of Eden for the first human was someone to love.

> The LORD God caused the man to fall into a deep sleep. While the man slept, the LORD God took out one of the man's ribs and closed up the opening. Then the LORD God made a woman from the rib, and he brought her to the man.
>
> "At last!" the man exclaimed.
>
> "This one is bone from my bone,
>   and flesh from my flesh!
> She will be called 'woman,'
>   because she was taken from 'man.'"
>
> This explains why a man leaves his father and mother and is joined to his wife, and the two are united into one.
>
> Now the man and his wife were both naked, but they felt no shame.[2]

The Bible calls those first two humans Adam and Eve, from the Hebrew words for "dirt" and "life," respectively. And the account of their first human love reveals three things that might be helpful.

First, Adam noted his *commonality* with Eve. "Bone from my bone!" he exclaimed. "Flesh from my flesh!" In other words, "We have so much in common!" The earth's first love poem exalts the commonality these two humans shared with each other—a realization that must have been all the more welcome after Adam had given names to all the animals,[3] an exercise that underscored his uniqueness, and aloneness, in creation. There were differences between the first and second humans on earth, to be sure—and still are, as many men and women can note—but it is significant that Adam's first expression of appreciation for his wife reflected the things that bound them together, the ways in which they were similar.

Next, the account refers to another basis on which true love is built—that of *community*. A man who falls in love and takes a wife "leaves his father and mother and is joined to his wife, and the two are united into one."[4] They pledge themselves to each other and form a new community. They not only combine their property, possessions, priorities, and problems into one—their *persons* are combined. The "two are united into one," the Bible says.

And, finally, those first pages of recorded human history reflect one more thing: *communion*. The account says "the man and his wife were both naked, but they felt no shame."[5] They were intertwined with each other, body and soul. Nothing was hidden. Nothing withheld. They enjoyed complete intimacy with each other and were unashamed to be seen and known so thoroughly.

Those are the things that make falling in love so fulfilling and rewarding. And they are the very things that make falling in love with God so satisfying.

The Greatest Love of All

The commonality, community, and communion that Adam and Eve experienced in the Garden are things every human soul longs for. And not only in our human relationships. God wants us to experience those things in our relationship with him.

The first mention of human beings in the Creation accounts depicts our commonality with God. "Let us make man in our image," he said, "after our likeness."[6] God's action in creating humankind is noticeably special, distinct from all the works of creation that preceded it. Gregory of Nyssa, writing in the fourth century, pointed out:

> O marvelous! a sun is made, and no counsel precedes;
> a heaven likewise; and to these no single thing in
> creation is equal. So great a wonder is formed by a
> word alone, and the saying indicates neither when, nor
> how, nor any such detail. So too in all particular cases,
> the æther, the stars, the intermediate air, the sea, the
> earth, the animals, the plants—all are brought into
> being with a word, while only to the making of man
> does the Maker of all draw near with circumspection,
> so as to prepare beforehand for him material for his
> formation, and to liken his form to an archetypal
> beauty, and, setting before him a mark for which
> he is to come into being, to make for him a nature
> appropriate and allied to the operations, and suitable
> for the object in hand.[7]

As human beings created in the image of God, we are unlike the rest of creation. There is a *commonality* between us and God, the spirit-life that God breathed into our first ancestor when, as the Bible records, "the LORD God formed man of the dust of the ground, and breathed into his nostrils the breath of life; and man became a living soul."[8] We are not bone of his bone or flesh of his flesh; we are something more. We are spirit of his Spirit.

More than that, however, God's design is for our relationship with him to be built on true *community*. It is why, when he rescued the Hebrews from slavery in Egypt, he set up his tent—the tabernacle—in the center of their encampment. It is why, when he gathered them together to teach them how to live in community with each other and with him, he told them, first and foremost, "Love the LORD your God with all your heart, all your soul, and all your strength."[9]

More than a thousand years later, Jesus called those words "the first and greatest commandment."[10] They are the sum and summit of what God desires *from* us and *for* us—not our obedience, primarily. Not fear. Not obligation or even admiration. He wants our love. He wants us to fall in love with him. He wants us to experience the rapture and reward that Adam felt when he walked with God in the Garden, in sweet and sinless companionship.

Ultimately, of course, God's hope and plan for us is to enter into *communion* with him, a relationship that is not all that different from Adam's and Eve's when they were intimate and unashamed. Communion with God is the spiritual reality that even the most fulfilling human relationships merely reflect. Just as Adam and Eve were depicted as becoming "one flesh," so the Apostle Paul wrote, "whoever is united with the Lord is one with him in spirit."[11] Every human soul—whether he or she knows it or not—desperately longs to be united with God in a real, loving relationship; one that is like that of husband and wife, but greater; one that is like that of parent and child, but stronger; one that is like that of friend to friend, but sweeter.

What our souls long for and what God wants for us is the same thing. We sense—and he knows—that it is possible. We suspect—and he supplies—the fulfillment and reward that accompanies it.

And he has even supplied us with a road map of sorts, a story that can help us find our way to the love that exceeds all understanding.[12]

That's the Way Love Goes

When Melissa asked that bold, honest question among her friends from church, the other people in the room were stymied momentarily, but not because they didn't know anything about loving God. On the contrary, some of the people in that group had been lovers of God for decades.

Back in the days before Garmin or other GPS devices, I would usually obtain something called a "Triptik" from my AAA Auto Club anytime I prepared for a long trip in my car. It was a handy, user-friendly tool for finding my way from here to there. But once the trip was over and I'd returned home, the Triptik went in the garbage. Once I made the trip, I didn't need to remember the route I took to get here or there.

I think that's pretty much how we tend to treat our spiritual journeys. Those of us who have fallen in love with God seldom save the directions. So if someone asks us, "How do you fall in love with God?" we suddenly realize that we don't remember the route we took to get there.

But someone has. And he wrote it down. His name was Hosea. He lived roughly three thousand years ago. He became something of an expert on falling in love with God. And his "Triptik" has been preserved for us in the ancient book of the Bible that bears his name.

The story of Hosea is one of the oldest—and most offbeat—romances in the history of literature. And it is all the more fascinating because it so happens that this fascinating book was intended—first for Hosea and then for Israel—to show exactly what Melissa was asking about. It is a true-life account of how to fall in love with God.

2

Who Wrote the
Book of Love?

I had a friend when I was a fairly young teenager (I've had one or two other friends since then, too). I'll call him Dave, instead of his real name, Joe, to protect his identity. Just kidding, his name wasn't Joe, either.

Dave had a crush on a pretty girl. One day, he summoned the courage to ask her for a date. She turned him down.

Dave knew—as pretty much everyone knew—that she was extremely shy. And I and his other friends assured Dave (when we weren't in an abusive mood) that he was actually a good-looking and accomplished guy, the kind most girls would find appealing. So there were good reasons for Dave to believe that her refusal stemmed from shyness and not some irrepressible revulsion toward him. So Dave stepped things up a bit. And by "a bit," I mean *infinitely*.

He launched a deliberate and concerted campaign to romance this girl into submission. He sent her flowers. He tied balloons to her school locker. He bought her candy—and not just candy, but a chocolate kiss the size of Rumania. When he learned the date of her birthday, he didn't just buy her a card and a gift; he put together thirty days of cards, baubles, tokens, gifts, and mementoes that were designed to systematically break down her resistance and turn her into his biggest fan.

It didn't work.

Seriously, I've never seen anything like it. He pulled out all the romantic stops, and she remained unmoved. The harder he tried, the worse it got, until her father eventually paid a call on Prince Charming and told him in no uncertain terms to back off.

Sure, Dave was guilty of overkill—but that was true in most things he did. Many girls would have been flattered at least, and convinced at best, by his tactics. Doesn't everyone want to be romanced? Don't we all want to be swept off our feet? Don't we all want to know that someone, somewhere, has noticed us and is willing to go to great lengths to win our attention, love, and devotion?

I know I do. I bet you do, too.

Hello, I Love You

To some extent, the entire Bible is about that very human, very common desire to love and be loved.

It can be said (and often has been said) that every book of the Bible is about God. Every chapter, every page, says something about him, about his nature, and about his love for us and his plans for us. And perhaps no book of the Bible says those things as clearly and powerfully as the Old Testament book of Hosea.

The ancient Scriptures which many people today call the Old Testament are organized into three parts in most Christian Bibles: History, Writings, and Prophets. The historical writings are also called "the Law" in Scripture because they contain the commands God gave his people; they extend from Genesis through Esther, charting human history and Israel's history from the world's creation to the end of Israel's captivity in Babylon. The Writings are the poetry and proverbs of God's people—Job, Psalms, Proverbs, Ecclesiastes, and the Song of Solomon. The Prophets comprise the rest of the Old Testament canon, seventeen books—some long, some short—of God's spokesmen, people like Isaiah and Ezekiel, Jonah and Jeremiah. The book of Hosea is the first of the twelve "minor prophets," so called not because their writings are unimportant but because they are much shorter than the prophecies of Isaiah, Jeremiah, Ezekiel, and Daniel.

The book of Hosea fits nicely in the flow of Israel's prophetic tradition. It was written at roughly the same time as the prophecies of Isaiah, Amos, Micah, and Obadiah. But it has its differences, too. Most importantly, Hosea is the first prophet in Israel's history to thoroughly and repeatedly depict God in terms of love.

Sure, God's people knew him to be a God of love long before Hosea's day. Way back in the days of the Exodus, Moses had told the people of Israel,

> "The LORD did not set his heart on you and choose
> you because you were more numerous than other
> nations, for you were the smallest of all nations!
> Rather, it was simply that the LORD loves you, and he
> was keeping the oath he had sworn to your ancestors.
> That is why the LORD rescued you with such a strong
> hand from your slavery and from the oppressive hand
> of Pharaoh, king of Egypt."[13]

And, as mentioned in Chapter One, God's people had early on been commanded to "love the LORD your God with all your heart, all your soul, and all your strength."[14] But generally speaking, God's relationship with his people for centuries had been defined by the prophets in terms of obedience and obligation, not in terms of love and affection.

But when God spoke to Hosea—and through him—he did so in strikingly new and unconventional terms.

Getting to Know You

The book of Hosea begins with a sort of preamble, like the scrolling screen that introduced the movie *Star Wars* ("Long, long ago in a galaxy far, far away"):

> The word of Yahweh came to a man named Hosea, the son of Beeri, back during the reigns of Uzziah, Jotham, Ahaz, and Hezekiah in Judah, and during the reign of Jeroboam the son of Joash in Israel.[15]

That short introduction gives us the context, the setting for all that follows.

First, it introduces us to the prophet who recorded this book of love. His name was Hosea, a fairly common name at the time, and one that means "God saves." It is the same name as Joshua, the warrior who took over the leadership of God's people after Moses's death, led the Israelites into the promised land, and helped them gain victory over their enemies. It is the same name as Hoshea, the last king of Israel.[16] It is the same name as Jeshua (or Joshua) the high priest, who returned from exile in Babylon with Nehemiah and Ezra and was portrayed as being graciously clothed in clean garments in a vision given to the prophet Zechariah.[17] And it is the same name as Jesus (or Y'shua), the spotless Lamb of God who would fulfill Zechariah's prophecy and remove the sin of all the people in a single day.[18] Hosea's name is probably not an accident or coincidence, because throughout the book of Hosea, he represents the love of God as it is revealed most powerfully in Jesus Christ.

That first verse of Hosea's prophecy also calls him "the son of Beeri." This identification is standard, of course, in a culture in which a man was distinguished primarily by his father's name. It must have meant something to the people who first received this prophecy—at the very least it must have distinguished him from "Hosea the son of Englebert" or "Hosea the son of Humperdink"— but it means virtually nothing to us today. Other than the meaning of the name in Hebrew (*Beeri* means "man of the well" or perhaps "keeper of the well"), we know nothing about Hosea's father or family. He may have been a farmer, as Hosea uses many agricultural references in his writing. He may have been a priest, given Hosea's familiarity with and passion for the priesthood. But we just don't know. Whatever fame or shame may have been attached to Hosea's family in his lifetime has been lost to us now.

The book's preamble also reveals that the word of the Lord came to Hosea "during the reigns of Uzziah, Jotham, Ahaz, and Hezekiah in Judah, and during the reign of Jeroboam the son of Joash in Israel."[19] This places Hosea's prophetic ministry in a specific time frame. He lived in the northern kingdom of Israel in the eighth century before the birth of Jesus. The descendants of Abraham, Isaac, and Jacob had for centuries been split into a northern kingdom, Israel, and a southern kingdom, Judah. Judah, depending on what king was leading them at the time, had sometimes followed God, and sometimes not. The northern kingdom, Israel—which couldn't claim a single righteous king in all their years of existence—had been following a spiraling path deeper and deeper into sin. Though it is by no means definite, Hosea probably grew up and prophesied in the northern kingdom, Israel, and spoke out as a prophet for at least twenty-five years, and perhaps for as long as sixty-five years.

This much we can know from that first verse of Hosea: His name. His father's name. His era. And not much else. Except for one more thing. The most important thing: the word of Yahweh came to him.

When You Spoke My Name

It's a straightforward phrase. Standard. The Bible says it repeatedly in relation to prophets:

> Then the word of the LORD came to Samuel.[20]

> That night the word of the LORD came to Nathan.[21]

> Then the word of the LORD came to Elijah.[22]

> Then the word of the LORD came to Isaiah.[23]

> Then the word of the LORD came to Jeremiah.[24]

> The word of the LORD came to Ezekiel the priest, the son of Buzi, by the Kebar River.[25]

> The word of the LORD came to Jonah son of Amittai.[26]

And so on. The phrase appears more than a hundred times in the Old Testament. It introduces the prophecies of Jonah and Zechariah, Isaiah and Ezekiel. And Hosea.

We don't know whether Hosea was his high school's prom king. We don't know whether he was the star of the local soccer team. We don't know whether he (or his father) had earned any distinction before that point. But it doesn't really matter. Whatever the facts of his life were up to that point, when Yahweh spoke to Hosea, that is what mattered from that point forward. And so it is with you.

Like Hosea, you may have a common name. You may not be famous. You may wonder why on earth you are on earth. But however famous or nonfamous—or even infamous—you may be at this moment, the past need not keep you from hearing the voice of Yahweh as you read these pages. It doesn't matter whether your name is Hosea or Hubert, Sharon or Shania; the word of the Lord can come to you and enter your heart and mind and soul. It can happen in the pages of this book. It can happen before you finish this chapter, if you will let it.

Likewise, your family history, your social status, income level, or reputation will also fade into the background when the word of the Lord comes to you. You may have been born into a family of great reputation, and you may be grateful and proud of your heritage. Good for you! Good for them! On the other hand, you may have been lucky to survive your upbringing. You may have experienced abandonment or abuse at the hands of those who should have loved you and helped you. You may not care to be known by your parents' name. In either case, the word of Yahweh can come to you. He can speak to you in spite of your family's glory as well as he can speak in spite of your family's shame. His voice can penetrate your groans of pain as well as your cries of triumph.

Neither can your era or environment deter the word of Yahweh from coming to you. Our modern world is filled with so many distractions that we may often find ourselves thinking it would be easier to hear God's voice and respond to it if we lived in an earlier age, when people rode horses instead of subway trains and talked around campfires instead of tweeting each other from across the room. You may be tempted to think that your setting is too busy or

27

too loud or too secular for God's voice to be heard. But he can speak to you, as he did to Hosea, regardless of your circumstances. He can come to you wherever you are. "The word of Yahweh came to a man named Hosea"[27] in an era of idolatry and oppression, at a time when practically no one around him seemed interested in hearing from God. Your era and your environment may not seem conducive to the voice of Yahweh, but it can hardly be less so than Hosea's.

One of my favorite authors, Samuel Logan Brengle, wrote these words:

> Mighty transformations are wrought in men by the
> coming of the word of the Lord to them! They can never
> more be the same men that they were before it came.
> It will either exalt them to the place of partners and
> co-workers with God, and give them a seat with Jesus on
> His throne, or it will banish them from His presence and
> doom them to hell. If obedient to the word, they will
> be saved, empowered, brought into closest fellowship
> with God, into confidential relations with Him, and
> they will be transformed into the likeness of His Son....
> It is the only way to true peace and highest usefulness
> here, and to endless glory and unfailing joy hereafter....
> Happy will you be if you have an ear to hear, a heart to
> understand, and the will to obey the word of the Lord.[28]

Like Hosea, anything and everything that can be known about you is unworthy of being compared to one, single, solitary fact: the word of the Lord has come to you. It is coming to you now. It is there, in the book of Hosea. And it is waiting to be discovered, personalized, and internalized by you.

3

Aligning
the Heart

The milkman Tevye's daughters had turned his world upside down. Rather than allowing Yente, the village matchmaker, to find them suitable husbands, Tevye's daughters informed him that they wanted to marry for love—unlike their father and mother, whose marriage had been arranged.

When Tevye tells his wife of their daughter Hodl's love for a penniless teacher, he muses that "it's a new world," in which daughters and sons prefer to fall in love before marrying each other. It wasn't how things were done in *his* day, but his daughters have started him thinking . . . and wondering. He turns to his wife of twenty-five years and asks, "Do you love me?"

"Do I what?!" she answers.

"Do you love me?"

"Do I love you?" she says, incredulously. "With our daughters getting married and trouble in the town, you're upset. You want out. Go inside. Go lie down. Maybe it's indigestion."

But Tevye presses the question.

"You're a fool," she says.

"I know," he answers. "But . . . do you love me?"

She echoes the question, and then says, "For twenty-five years I've washed your clothes, cooked your meals, cleaned your house, given you children, milked the cow. After twenty-five years, why talk about love right now?"

He recalls when they married. How his parents promised he and his bride would learn to love each other. So he asks her again whether she loves him, until finally she admits, "For twenty-five years I've lived with him, fought with him, starved with him; for twenty-five years my bed is his. If that's not love, what is?"

The song ends with the old married couple singing together, "It doesn't change a thing, but even so—after twenty-five years, it's nice to know."

That classic scene appears in the play and movie, *Fiddler on the Roof,* which is based on the stories of the great Yiddish writer Sholem Aleichem. And it depicts a perspective of love that is common among our Jewish friends, neighbors, and forebears—and one that is key to falling in love with God.

Why I Love You

Every one of us who falls in love—whether it is before the wedding or after twenty-five years—does so because we see something love-worthy in the object of our love. It may be striking good looks or a winsome sense of humor. It may be courage or compassion. It may be any number of things; but the spark that ignites love into a flicker, then a flame, is the recognition that there is some quality worth loving in the other.

But that's apparently not how Hosea's love story began. Instead, it starts out this way:

> When Yahweh first began speaking through Hosea, he told him, "I want you to go and marry a whore. Have children with her, to demonstrate what my people have done by forsaking Yahweh."[29]

Once upon a time in a kingdom far, far away, God told a man named Hosea to find a whore and marry her. Not much of a fairy tale, is it?

Now, let me say, first of all, I didn't choose the word "whore." It's a terrible word. But it's there, in the Bible. In fact, the language of the Hebrew text is clearly intended to stun and offend us. In some Bible translations, it's easy to miss the utterly shocking nature of God's words. But a few versions get closer to the impact of the original language:

"Go and marry a harlot." (Phillips)
"Go and marry a prostitute." (NLT)
"Find a whore and marry her." (*The Message*)

Oh my. Oh my.

Can you *imagine*? I mean, it's one thing just to hear from God. But can you imagine hearing God say, "Go, look up the sleaziest woman you can find and get hitched?"

What would *you* do? I mean, God is God, right? When he says, "Jump," we're supposed to say, "How high?"—especially if we're supposed to be a prophet. But still . . . dude! That's harsh!

Now, to be fair, we're not given a whole lot of background to the story. The phrasing of that verse in the original language makes it clear that the instruction to take a less-than-virginal wife was among the earliest—perhaps even *the first*—things God spoke to the prophet. If it had been me, I sure would have preferred a little time to get used to the whole process of hearing God speak, you know? It would have been nice to have a few "test messages" first, like "take that job at the supermarket" or "help that old lady across the street." Pretty much anything would have been a better introduction to the prophetic task than "go and marry a whore."

I also have to believe there are parts of the story that ended up, like many film scenes, on the cutting room floor. You know, was Hosea's first response "say what?" or "come again?" Did Hosea have a mother to explain things to? Or a girlfriend? We don't know. We're not told. The Bible simply says, next,

> So Hosea did just that. He went and found Gomer,
> the daughter of Diblaim. He married her, and she got
> pregnant by him and gave him a son.[30]

Again, there are so many blanks I wish had been filled in for us. We don't know whether Hosea already knew Gomer, to some extent. (And, by the way, if you're a baby boomer, you can just stop picturing Gomer Pyle. This Gomer probably looked nothing like Jim Nabors). Maybe they already had a relationship. Maybe Hosea had suspected her unfaithfulness and had cried out to God, brokenhearted, wondering if he should break things off, when God answered by saying, basically, "She is promiscuous, but I want you to marry her—even though she will further break your heart."

Or maybe not. Maybe Hosea strolled through the red light district saying, "No . . . no . . . not her . . . not that one . . . YES!" Maybe God caused a bright star to hover over one woman's head. Or perhaps Hosea just walked up to some lady of the evening and said, "Hi, you don't know me, but God told me to marry you" (guys, this is almost never a good pickup line). We're not told whether Hosea had to woo her, taking her out for drinks and a donkey race one night and dinner and a dance the next.

Yvonne Lehman, in her novel *In Shady Groves*[31] imagines Hosea as a young man who is pledged to be married to a good Jewish girl when he meets and falls in love with the beautiful Gomer, a girl from a nearby village. Only later does he discover that she is a prostitute at the temple of Baal in Bethel and that God is leading him to marry her. Was that how it happened? We just don't know. It doesn't say.

We don't even know whether Hosea doubted the word of the Lord. We don't know whether he vacillated. We don't know whether he argued with family and friends over the decision. We don't know whether he obeyed instantly or whether it took him weeks, or even months, to comply with God's command.

We simply know that Hosea, a prophet of God, actually married a prostitute because God told him to. Why would God do that? Why would he give Hosea such a weird command? Great question. And the answer, though it will be a while yet before we can fully grasp it, is all about how to fall in love with God.

You're Having My Baby

Poor Hosea. Other judges and prophets got to play the hero. Samson brought down the house. Nathan blew the whistle. Elijah rode a chariot of fire. But Hosea's prophetic career started with a really awkward wedding, one that was probably worse than the flakiest reality TV show.

And then, perhaps while he was still trying to figure out how to be a husband, Hosea became a father:

[Gomer] got pregnant by him and gave birth to a son.

When the boy was born, Yahweh told Hosea, "Name him Jezreel [meaning 'God will scatter'], for I will soon punish King Jehu and his royal house for the blood he shed in Jezreel, and I will abolish the kingdom of Israel. I will break Israel's military power in the Valley of Jezreel."[32]

Now, in Hebrew culture, just like in Native American culture, parents gave their babies names that *meant* something—like Hosea's name, remember, which meant "the Lord saves" or "the Lord is my salvation." But here, God tells Hosea to name his son Jezreel, which meant, literally, "God scatters" or "God sows," but had come to be a synonym for "castaway." "Unwanted." "Reject."

D. Stuart Briscoe, in his book *Taking God Seriously*, explains the heavy meaning behind the name:

> The very name, Jezreel, would take the people back in their minds to the time of a particularly obnoxious king and queen, Ahab and Jezebel. Though they had plenty of property of their own, they coveted the vineyard of Naboth, a Jezreelite farmer. This man's vineyard, which had been handed down from generation to generation, unfortunately adjoined Ahab's palace at Jezreel, and the king wanted it badly. His evil wife Jezebel plotted how to get the land from Naboth. By hiring false witnesses against the farmer, she got the land for Ahab and had Naboth stoned to death. For her evil actions, Jezebel came under the judgment of God and later died a horrible death at the hands of Jehu. In his own time, Jehu came under God's judgment and he, too, died

and was buried in Samaria. Jeroboam II came from the stock of Jezreel, Jezebel, and Jehu, and he, too, lived a life that was utterly repugnant to God. For that reason, the name Jezreel, given in Israel at the time of Hosea, would be a constant reminder of a time in Israel's history that was abhorrent to God. Hosea's son is a reminder of Jezreel's sad, bloody history.[33]

Poor kid.

You thought it was tough growing up with *your* name? Try growing up with the name "Abhorrent." Or "Reject." Ouch.

There was a divine reason, however, for such an unfortunate name. God chose it as a way of warning Israel that their wicked leadership would soon be destroyed and the whole nation would soon be rejected because of their sin. But the drama is just beginning.

Baby, Baby

The story continues in verses 6–9:

> Sometime later, Gomer got pregnant again and gave birth to a daughter. And Yahweh told Hosea, "Name her Lo-ruhamah [meaning 'Unloved'], for I am through showing love to Israel, I am done forgiving them. I will show love to Judah, and deliver them from their enemies—but I'll make it clear that neither firepower nor strategy has saved them, but only Yahweh, their God."
>
> When Gomer had weaned Unloved, she became pregnant again and had another child, a son. And Yahweh said, "Give him the name, Lo-ammi [meaning 'Not Mine'] because Israel is not my people, and I am not your God."[34]

Notice what's happening here. Gomer has two more children. But the Bible uses different phrasing to refer to those two births. In the case of Jezreel, the account says this:

> She got pregnant by him and gave birth to a son.[35]

The text makes it clear that Hosea fathered the child. But the second and third time around, it doesn't say that. It says:

> Gomer got pregnant again and gave birth to a daughter.[36]

And,

> She became pregnant again and had another child, a son.[37]

In the case of their first child, the Bible says that Hosea is the father. And in the case of the second and third births, the account says simply that she becomes pregnant and has a child. *Gomer* has a child. But apparently not Hosea.

Jezreel is his son. Lo-ruhamah and Lo-ammi, maybe not so much.

Oh my. Can you imagine how Hosea felt?

Out of obedience to God, he had married this woman who was a *prostitute*—and perhaps, judging from her name, which means "consummate," the worst of the worst, the whorest of the whores, so to speak. She was No One. She had nothing. And Hosea took her home and took her in, made her his wife, and bestowed his name on her. And she betrayed him in the worst possible way.

And not once.

It wasn't a "mistake," a moment of weakness. It wasn't a fleeting lapse in judgment.

He had made her a bride . . . but she had made him a cuckold, a fool.

So God tells Hosea to name the children Lo-ruhamah, or "Unloved," and Lo-ammi, "Not Mine," names that drive home the tragic results of Gomer's unfaithfulness to Hosea.

It's a story we could call "The Prophet and the Prostitute," a story of heartbreak, betrayal, and agony. It's a story that makes us ask again, "Why?" Why would God ask such things of poor Hosea? Why would he command this poor man to take a prostitute for a wife? Why would he tell him to give such awful names to his poor children? Why would he let Hosea suffer such undeserving heartbreak?

If you can understand the answer to that, you can start to trace the route to falling in love with God. Why did God ask such things of Hosea? So he would understand—not only in his head, but also in his heart, in his *gut*, through his own experience, the scandal of God's love for him, for Israel, for you.

Because, you see, one key to falling in love with God is *experiencing* the scandal of God's love for you. God didn't ask Hosea to proclaim his love, to prophecy his love, to preach about his love, until Hosea had tasted on a human scale the extent of God's condescension.

God condescended to me in spite of my shame

God told Hosea to go and marry a whore.

Can you even imagine what that was like? For Hosea to leave his cozy suburban bungalow to go to the seedy, sleazy red light district, to a woman who had slept with two or three men the night before . . . and in the light of day with mocking eyes watching, ask her to be his wife?

This is no pretty scene out of a Julia Roberts movie. Only the ugliest, most sordid, most revolting and shameful condescension imaginable could even begin to put Hosea's heart in touch with the inconceivable distance between God's holiness and their filthiness. Only something that dramatic could demonstrate how far Yahweh would condescend, what he would do, for his bride. For me. For you.

Perhaps you have heard or read the story of an early Christ-follower, the woman who had been caught in adultery and was dragged in front of Jesus so his enemies could use her to trap him.

You may remember that, after he confounded them by saying simply, "If any one of you is without sin, let him be the first to throw a stone at her," they all left, one by one.

And you may recall that when they were all gone and this adulterous woman was left alone with him, he said,

> "Woman, where are they? Has no one condemned you?"
> "No one, sir," she said.
> "Then neither do I condemn you," Jesus declared. "Go now and leave your life of sin."[38]

Do you know that he addressed her with the same term of respect he used with his own mother?

"Woman . . ."
"Ma'am . . ."

Do you know how far God condescended to be able to speak terms of love and respect . . . to you?

Do you know that he set aside majesty and glory, riches and comfort, to be able to say,

> There is . . . no condemnation for those who are in Christ Jesus.[39]

Do you know that the amount of condescension involved in the infinite, eternal God entering time and space for *you* is *immeasurable*?

Do you know that he comes to you even in your shame?

Do you know that no matter how low you may feel you're not too low for him to reach?

The psalmist said,

> If I make my bed in the depths, you are there.[40]

Oh, the depth of the mercy of God! That he would condescend to me—to you—no matter how low we go, no matter how shameful we may feel, that he would condescend so far to us that Hosea had to marry a prostitute to even begin to grasp it.

Not only that, but Hosea's experience also shows us the scandal of God's love in overcoming our past.

God chose me in spite of my past

My wife, the lovely Robin, is a fan of western movies. They don't even have to be good. So when the Kevin Costner movie *Open Range* came out, I took her to see it. In the film, Costner plays a hard-case "free range" cowboy who meets a woman, a doctor's sister, played by Annette Bening. Costner's character is attracted to her. But he holds back. He seems almost frightened of her. And at one point he reveals why: he's afraid that if she knew his past she would be scared. Or repulsed. Or both. It's clear that his past is ugly, violent, and vile.

When you've got a lot of garbage in your past, it's hard to believe someone would choose you. That's what victims of abuse, addiction, and rape struggle with. They find it hard to believe someone could ever choose them if they knew all there was to know.

That was probably what happened when Hosea married Gomer, the daughter of Diblaim. The Bible doesn't tell us, but if I had to guess, I'd say Hosea's wife was the worst of the worst—no *Pretty*

Woman, not at all—but the woman with the worst reputation, the worst past (which, as I said a few pages back, would have been in keeping with her name). Because only by marrying her could Hosea's heart be put in touch with what God would do for me. Only in such a way could God demonstrate his plan to choose you in spite of your past.

Maybe you haven't responded to his overtures. Maybe you've never surrendered to his overcoming love. If that is the case, I hope that's something you can do right now, right here, by praying a simple prayer of faith, like this:

> *Jesus, you see into my heart right now.*
> *You know the things in my life, in my past,*
> *that have hurt me and brought me shame.*
> *You know everything I've done, the good and the bad.*
> *And you love me anyway.*
> *You call me to yourself.*
> *You condescend to me.*
> *You know all there is to know about me, yet you want me to*
>   *be yours.*
> *I lay before you all my sins,*
> *and on the basis of your sacrifice on the cross,*
> *I ask you to forgive me,*
> *wash my heart clean,*
> *and enter into my heart and life,*
> *to dwell there and control my life from this day forward.*
>   *In Jesus' name, amen.*

If you sincerely prayed that prayer—or something like it, no matter how long ago—Paul, the great church planter of the first century, described your life's reality when he wrote the following words to the church in Corinth:

> Do you not know that the wicked will not inherit the kingdom of God? Do not be deceived: Neither the sexually immoral nor idolaters nor adulterers nor male prostitutes nor homosexual offenders nor thieves nor the greedy nor drunkards nor slanderers nor swindlers will inherit the kingdom of God. *And that is what some of you were.* But you were washed, you were sanctified, you were justified in the name of the Lord Jesus Christ and by the Spirit of our God.[41]

Oh, if you and I could fully realize that, despite our past—despite the abuse we suffered, despite the self-loathing we felt, despite the crummy choices we made, despite our sin, despite the family we had, despite our failures and flaws—God in Christ chose us. "You did not choose me," Jesus said, "but I chose you."[42]

We talk about choosing Christ. We sing, "I have decided to follow Jesus," and that's certainly how it looks from our perspective. But from the Bible's perspective—and from Hosea's perspective—it looks more like this:

> You were dead in your transgressions and sins . . . gratifying the cravings of [your] sinful nature and following its desires and thoughts. . . .
>
> But because of his great love for [you], God, who is rich in mercy, made [you] alive with Christ even when [you] were dead in transgressions—it is by grace you have been saved.[43]

Getting into Hosea's story ought to prompt us to fall in love with God, who is rich in mercy and abounding in grace toward us, as we realize his unfathomable, immeasurable condescension to find us and save us and make us his bride, in spite of our shame, in spite of our past.

God loves me in spite of my betrayal

The Bible talks about "how wide and long and high and deep is the love of Christ."[44] It is a poetic phrase. A beautiful image. But just how deep *is* the love of Christ?

It's this deep: Remember Lo-ruhamah and Lo-ammi? Hosea had to experience what it was like to watch his wife bear another man's children, to taste that bitter betrayal, *and love her anyway* in order to begin to understand how deep the love of God is.

It's this deep: Remember Judas? Jesus knew when he ate his last supper in the Upper Room with his followers that Judas had already betrayed him. But rather than expose him or banish him, Jesus washed his feet and dipped a piece of bread in the bowl of oil and herbs and gave it to Judas, a sign of hospitality and friendship that persists even to this day in Eastern lands.[45]

It's this deep: Remember Peter? On the last night of his life, Jesus warned that Peter would deny him before the next morning dawned, and Peter did . . . vehemently. But when Jesus rose from the dead and appeared to Peter and the other disciples, he cooked him breakfast one morning by the sea and communicated his widelong-highdeep love by giving Peter a chance to renew his love for Jesus as many times as he had earlier denied it.[46]

Of course, Judas hung himself, and so missed that kind of forgiveness and restoration. Ever wonder why? Why one man who betrayed Jesus' love for him let his betrayal destroy him, while another who had vehemently denied him found forgiveness and restoration?

I have a guess. Maybe it was so we can see the contrast . . . and be warned by it.

Oh, I don't know about you, but I have many times betrayed God's love for me, no less than a wife who bears another man's child.

I have slept with the Enemy.

I have eaten at God's table and then, just hours later, betrayed him as boldly as Judas.

I have failed him by the fires of unbelievers no less than Peter.

And I'm so tempted to run from him like Judas—and so condemn myself. But if, instead, like Peter I shed my inhibitions and baggage and race—or swim[47]—to my waiting Savior, I will find not rejection, but reconciliation, mercy, grace, and love.

Head Over Heels

In spite of all the unfaithfulness and betrayal and spiritual adultery of Israel, the first chapter of Hosea concludes with a striking promise:

> Still [God says], there will come a day when the people of Israel will be as numerous as sands on the seashore. In the very place where they were named "Not Mine" they will be called "God's Own." And the people of Judah and of Israel will be reunited, as one, under One. What a day of rejoicing that will be, a day of exaltation, the day of Jezreel,
>
> when you tell your brothers, "You are my flesh and blood," and say to your sisters, "You have been shown mercy."[48]

Through his obliging prophet Hosea, God promises these people who had betrayed him like an adulterous wife that there will nonetheless come a day when *Lo-ammi*—"Not Mine"—will become *bar El chai*—"God's Own" (literally "sons of the Living God").

That's the kind of God you can fall in love with. If you, like Hosea, can somehow grasp that he condescended to you in spite of your shame, chose you in spite of your past, and loves you unconditionally in spite of your betrayal, then you may be on your way. If you can let the scandal of God's love for you enter not only into your head but into your heart as well, then you may soon—perhaps before finishing this book—find yourself falling head over heels in love with God.

———————— ⸙ ————————

God, you really did condescend to me, didn't you? You chose me. You love me unconditionally. In spite of anything and everything, Lord, you care so much for me that you had your prophet Hosea marry a prostitute to show how wide and long and high and deep your love is for me.

It's hard to really feel "in touch" with that kind of love. But if you'll help me, God, I would like to understand—not only in my head, but in my heart, in my gut, through my own experience, the splendid and terrible scandal of your love for me. Amen.

4

Awaking
to Love

Inception *was a 2010 science* fiction film written, coproduced, and directed by Christopher Nolan of *Batman Begins* fame. It told the story of Dom Cobb, played by Leonardo DiCaprio, a corporate spy whose task it is to secretly extract information from people's dreams. Cobb is hired by a businessman named Saito (played by Ken Watanabe) to do what many believed to be impossible: to plant an original idea in the mind of a subject, something called "inception." In order to do that, Cobb and his team have to not only enter the dreams of their subject; they have to delve into the dream within a dream—and the dream within that one—and plant the idea as deeply as possible in the person's subconscious to ensure that it takes root.

Many fans of the movie found the concept fascinating—that is, the idea that a sleeping person could be dreaming, and in their dream they could be asleep and dreaming yet another dream, and so on—like the various parts of a Russian nesting doll or the multiple reflections in a house of mirrors, extending (in theory) to infinity.

Something like that is happening in the book of Hosea. It tells the story of Hosea and his marriage to Gomer. But wrapped up in Hosea's marriage is another story: the tale of God's love for his wayward people, Israel. And inside that romance are still more: Your story. And mine. And everyone's, to one extent or another.

After the Love Has Gone

God had told his prophet Hosea to marry a "whore" and set up housekeeping with her to mirror God's own relationship with his people, Israel. Briscoe helps us understand why:

> God had revealed himself to his people. When they came into the land of Canaan, they were told to worship Jehovah exclusively. The worship of the Canaanite gods could not exist alongside the worship of Jehovah. But what happened? As soon as they reached Canaan, they began to intermarry with the Canaanites. They began to assimilate Canaanite religion. In no time they began to lust after the idols of the Canaanites. So bad did this idolatry become that Jeroboam I, when he became king of Israel, breaking away from the southern kingdom of Judah, said, "'It is too much for you to go up to Jerusalem. Here are your gods, O Israel, who brought you up out of Egypt'" (1 Kings 12:28). The "gods" he made were two golden calves, similar to those used in Baal worship. He told the people that they should simply worship the calves he set up in the two strategic cities of Bethel and Dan. Worship became a matter of convenience, a matter of identifying with the culture, a matter of simply doing things their own way rather than God's way.[49]

Both figuratively and literally, Israel had prostituted herself. Not only had the people turned away from God—their true husband—but they had also turned to Baal, a Canaanite deity whose worship involved unbridled sexual activity with temple prostitutes.

We don't know, of course, but that may have been how Gomer twice got pregnant by someone other than Hosea. Even then, however, the story wasn't over. The second chapter of the book that bears Hosea's name begins (after the first verse, which is best understood as a concluding phrase to chapter 1) with words that sound like an ancient divorce decree.

In ancient Israel, a man divorced his wife by having a document drawn up, called a *get*, which stated that she was no longer his wife. The divorce was finalized when the husband delivered the *get* into her hands.

Some scholars recognize the first words of Hosea 2 as a formal declaration of divorce. It may be that Hosea, having suffered long and deeply through his wife's repeated betrayals, finally delivered a *get* to her. It may have been that development in the story of Hosea that forms the background for the words God speaks in Hosea 2, which begin with an echo of a divorce decree:

> "Persuade your mother, beg her—
>> for she is no wife to me,
>> and I am no longer her husband—
> that she stop whoring around,
>> and wipe away her adulterous makeup and perfume;
> or I will strip her myself,
>> naked as the day she was born,
>> remove all her pretenses
>> and expose her to utter desolation and emptiness.

And I won't stop there. I will show no mercy to
   her children,
      because they are the children
      of her whorish behavior.
She has brought shame on them,
      running after her lovers
      for the ease and the comforts they provide,
      bread and water,
      wool and flax, oil and drink.
So I will block her way with a thorny hedgerow.
      I will wall her off from her wayward paths,
so that when she heads out for a rendezvous,
      she will fail
      and won't even be able to find her lovers.
Then she will have to return to her husband,
      to a time when things were better for her."[50]

Even as God's heart is breaking, his purpose and plan are redemptive. Even as he announces his separation from his beloved, he says it is intended to change her mind, to change her ways. His purpose in exposing her "to utter desolation and emptiness" is to wake her up. His plan in showing no mercy to her children, in "blocking her way with a thorny hedgerow" and walling her off "from her wayward paths," is that "she will have to return to her husband"—to him.

Do You Want to Know a Secret?

Another echo of Hosea's love for Gomer may be seen in the next verses of chapter 2. Even after she betrayed him, bearing two children that belonged to other men, Hosea apparently cared for his wife. In fact, there is evidence that after she left his home and took up with other men, he continued to surreptitiously provide for her:

> "She doesn't even know
>> that all along I was the one
>> giving her grain, wine, and oil.
> I was the one who made sure she was taken care of,
>> while she would just spend my gifts on others."[51]

We don't know how Hosea managed it. Maybe he arranged for goods to be delivered to her door. Maybe he replenished her pantry when she was out of the house. Maybe he paid her bills when local merchants threatened to cut her off. But the text indicates that Hosea's generosity kept flowing to his beloved even after her many betrayals.

Like a dream within a dream, Hosea's story is God's story, too. Or vice versa. Centuries before, God had warned his people through Moses:

> Be careful that you do not forget the LORD your God,
> failing to observe his commands, his laws and his
> decrees that I am giving you this day. Otherwise, when
> you eat and are satisfied, when you build fine houses
> and settle down, and when your herds and flocks grow
> large and your silver and gold increase and all you have
> is multiplied, then your heart will become proud and
> you will forget the LORD your God, who brought you
> out of Egypt, out of the land of slavery.[52]

But despite the warning, written and recorded in the venerated Law of Moses, they did exactly that. And yet still, long after Israel turned away and pursued other gods and other priorities, God continued to send rain, grain, wine, and oil on the land. He continued to provide for his people. He took care of them, much as Hosea took care of Gomer—faithfully and constantly.

But like Gomer, Israel never acknowledged what they owed to God's care. No gratitude for life. No thanks for rain. No worship at harvest time. They spent the blessings he sent on other lovers. So God—perhaps guiding his prophet to do the same—determines to show "tough love" to his beloved:

> "So now I will take back my grain when it's ripe,
>   and my wine when it's ready.
> I will repossess my wool and my flax,
>   which were intended to cover her with warmth
>   and respectability.
> Now, instead, I will expose her
>   while all her so-called lovers look on,
>   and no one will claim her from me.
> I will shut down all her partying,
>   her feasts, and dances, and holidays.
> And I will level her gardens and orchards,
>   which she claimed as her right,
>   and counted as payment from her lovers.
> I will turn them back into wilderness,
>   fit only for wild animals.
> I will punish her for all her festivals to Baal,
>   when she offered sacrifices to her idols
> and bedecked herself with makeup and jewels for her lovers
>   and forgot me,"
> says Yahweh.[53]

When a man divorced his wife in ancient Israel, the *get* indicated that she was free to belong to someone else. The plan God outlines in the verses above, however, is not intended to result in him being forever rid of his beloved; the idea is to reclaim her for himself. He (and presumably Hosea as well) announces that all his provision and care will be stopped, and she will be left in such a state that "no one will claim her from me." Though she will be bereft, the purpose of her bereavement is her reclamation, a plan that becomes even clearer and brighter in the final verses of Hosea 2.

Beautiful Dreamer

Sometimes, in Hosea's prophecy it is hard for the reader to know who is speaking, and which story is being told: Hosea's or God's. That's because the answer is usually, "both." And, as mentioned earlier, those two levels of understanding can be understood as also previewing others: yours and mine. So it is in the beautiful vision Hosea 2:15–23 presents:

> "But I will woo her again.
>> I will take her out into the wilderness,
>> and romance her with words.
> I will give her back her vineyards
>> and turn her Valley of Trouble into a Doorway
>>> of Hope.
> And she will respond to me as she did when she was young,
>> when I brought her out of slavery in Egypt.
>
> "And then, Israel," Yahweh says,
>> "you will call me 'my husband'
>> instead of just 'my master.'
> I will make her forget the Baals;
>> I will make their names foreign to her lips.
> And on that day I will make a peace treaty

with the wild animals and birds,
    the rodents and reptiles,
and abolish the weapons of war from the land,
        so you can lie down in perfect peace and safety.
And I will bind you to me forever
    with bands of righteousness and justice,
        of unwavering love and mercy.
I will be your faithful husband,
    and you will truly know me.

"And then I will answer,"
    Yahweh says,
"and speak to the heavens,
        and they will grant the earth's requests for rain,
and the earth will hear the thirsty cries of grain,
        wine, and oil,
        and restore plenty to Jezreel.
I will shower my love on Unloved,
        and I will say to Not Mine,
'You are mine.' And he will answer me,
        'You are my God.'"[54]

Like the mind-boggling levels of dreams in the movie *Inception*, those words from Hosea's second chapter not only reflect the course of the prophet's struggles with his wayward wife and God's journey with his wayward people; they can also be understood as a mini-manual for anyone today who would fall in love with God. Because what was true of Hosea and of Israel is true also of you—and me and the whole human race. It ought to open our eyes to a few striking realities, even as it sketches three necessary steps to the kind of love relationship with God for which our hearts long.

I admit my fundamental fallenness

For Hosea—a prophet of God, under instruction from Yahweh himself—to present his wife with a divorce decree, as apparently described in Hosea 2:2, could have been no small thing. He was a man of God! He had married the woman at God's behest! And yet, after her repeated unfaithfulness, Hosea decreed, "she is no wife to me, and I am no longer her husband."[55] We are not told, but I can only imagine that it was far more than an embarrassment to Hosea. It must have been devastating and absolutely humiliating. Looking back on it, we may be able to see how necessary it was in God's plan to get through to his people, but it still could not have been anything less than tragic for Hosea.

Eons before, God had suffered a parallel devastation, when the man and woman he had lovingly created and placed in the Garden of Eden had flagrantly betrayed his love and care and done the one thing they must have known would break his heart. We are not told much of God's reaction to their betrayal—we don't even know how long it took them to tire of perfection and paradise before succumbing to sin. We don't know whether they had enjoyed perfect intimacy with God for a week or a decade before trusting the serpent's words more than God's. But it takes very little imagination to hear God's heart breaking in the Genesis 3 account of him searching for his loved ones in the Garden, as they hid from him. That betrayal was followed by a divorce of sorts, as God pronounced a decree and sent his loved ones from their garden home—a separation that long outlived the first man and the first woman.

But we all know—Adam and Eve weren't the only ones. Every soul since then has signed up for the rebellion, some of us earlier and some of us later than others, perhaps. But every one of us reached a place of decision early in our lives, a place where we faced a choice between right and wrong, between righteousness and unrighteousness. And we chose wrong. We chose unrighteousness. We sinned. And not just once.

Years ago, my friend Jim, who is a gifted personal evangelist, told me how he relates to a people who have trouble admitting to being sinners.

"Our sinful nature," Jim said, "makes it hard for us to admit our sinful nature. So when I sense that a person is struggling with the concept of sin in their lives, I'll say something like, 'I bet you have pretty high standards.' The person will almost always say that they do. So then I'll say, 'What are some of those standards you expect of other people?' At that, the person will often say, 'Oh, I expect people to be completely truthful and honest in their dealings with me. And to be kind in the way they treat other people. And to work hard and give more than they take.'

"The specifics differ at times," Jim said, "but the gist is always the same. So then I'll say something like, 'So, do you always live up to those standards?' And the person will say, 'Most of the time.' 'Good for you,' I'll say, before asking, 'But not all the time?' 'Well, no,' the answer will always come back, 'not all the time.' And then I'll nod in understanding and say, 'So you don't always live up to your own standards.' They'll usually agree with a shrug, before I say, 'Would you expect God's standards to be higher than yours?' Of course, everyone agrees to that, and that's when I'll point out, 'If you're able to admit that you don't even live up to your own standards, and God probably has higher standards than you, do you think it's possible that you don't live up to God's standards? In fact, do you think maybe you fall short of God's standards even more than you fall short of your own?'"

I would think any honest person would have to be persuaded by that line of reasoning. Yet many of us skip blithely through our lives with little understanding of how fallen we truly are. We are not like the store cashier who comes up a penny or two short when counting the receipts in the cash register at the end of a day; we are much more like the Wall Street villain who bilked retirees out of their pensions so he could live a life of luxury.

Does that seem too harsh?

Think about it, though. Like everyone else on this earth, I was created by a loving God who didn't have to create me. He didn't owe me an existence. My every breath is a gift. Every single heartbeat is a grace. My circumstances may be far from perfect, but God never owed me a moment's attention. And yet here I am.

But also, like everyone else, I have repeatedly tried to seize the crown God wears and become sovereign of my own life, captain of my own fate. Like Adam and Eve, I have thought it better to take things into my own hands. I have chosen wrong, time and time again. I have ignored his whisperings. I have been too busy for his attentions. I have made him wait. I have spurned him.

Worse, like Gomer, I have pursued other lovers. He made my heart for his. He created me to find fulfillment only in his embrace. But I looked for approval from mere mortals. I sought security in money. I pursued fulfillment in food and entertainment. I ran after other lovers "for the ease and the comforts they provide."[56]

So much of what God has done—or allowed—in my life and in yours has been for the purpose of waking us up to the breadth and depth of our repeated, unfeeling rejection of him. And so much of his message through Hosea is intended for the very same purpose.

I acknowledge God's unwavering care

"Don't it always seem to go," suggested the prophet Joni, "that you don't know what you've got till it's gone?"[57] We often fail to appreciate God's unwavering care for us until we sense—or fear—its absence.

Just like ancient Israel, I have habitually taken for granted God's kindness and generosity toward me. He created my inmost being; he knitted together all my parts while I was still in my mother's womb.[58] He formed not only my body but my spirit, as well. He has invested thought and attention in me from day one.

How many healthy days have I passed in this body without thanking God for that health? Yet the moment a virus strikes or an infection lays me low, I turn to God for relief.

How many checks have I written, how many bills have I paid, without pausing to acknowledge the God who gave me the ability to produce wealth?[59] Yet when the cupboard is nearly bare and the bank account is nearly empty, I once again turn my attention to the One who "sends poverty and wealth."[60]

How many blessings have I enjoyed without acknowledging that they came from God? How many fresh starts have I been given? How many laughs? How many restful nights? How many hugs and kisses from loved ones? How many good books? Fine meals? Gentle breezes? How many beautiful sights? How many musical sounds? How many pleasant smells and tender touches?

David McIntyre, in his classic book *The Hidden Life of Prayer* suggests,

> Let us take trouble to observe and consider the
> Lord's dealings with us, and we shall surely receive
> soul-enriching views of His kindness and truth.

His mercies are new every morning. He makes the outgoings of the evening to rejoice. His thoughts concerning us are for number as the sands on the shore, and they are all thoughts of peace. Those benefits which recur with so much regularity that they seem to us "common" and "ordinary," which penetrate with golden threads the homespun vesture of our daily life, ought to be most lovingly commemorated. For, often, they are unspeakably great. "I have experienced today the most exquisite pleasure I have ever had in my life," said a young invalid; "I was able to breathe freely for about five minutes."[61]

Or, to use God's imagery in the book of his prophet Hosea, how much grain have I eaten? How much wine and oil have I poured? How much wool and flax have covered me with warmth and respectability? What gardens and orchards have I known? What feasts and holidays? What makeup and jewels? What comforts and luxuries have I accepted, imagining or pretending that I deserve them all, while in reality they have come to me as gifts from the Lover of my soul?

Like Hosea's unfaithful wife and God's ungrateful Israel, it usually takes a shock or a shortage to remind me that "every good and perfect gift is from above, coming down from the Father."[62] How consistently and constantly have I grieved my heavenly Father by forgetting that all I am and all I have come from him? How often, when he was the one who made sure I was taken care of, did I thoughtlessly—even willfully—spend his gifts on other loves, including myself?[63] And how patient has he been, day by day, week by week, month by year by decade, to withhold judgment and wait for me to come to my senses—and not just one time, but repeatedly? What a gracious Lover he is, to patiently endure my thoughtless neglect, my rude forgetfulness.

I awake to the depth of my need

The 2012 movie *The Vow*, starring Rachel McAdams and Channing Tatum, was based on the real-life experience of Kim and Krickitt Carpenter. Just two months after he had married the woman of his dreams, a devastating auto accident left his bride in a coma, suffering from a massive head injury. When she began the long, slow process of recovery from her coma, she spoke only in one- or two-syllable responses to questions, and these came only after long pauses. Eventually, however, her therapist began to probe a little more, as her husband relates:

> "Krickitt," her therapist began in a soothing voice, "do you know where you are?"
>
> Krickitt thought for a minute before replying. "Phoenix."
>
> "That's right, Krickitt. Do you know what year it is?"
> "1965."
>
> *She was born in 1969,* I thought, somewhat frantically. *That's just a little setback—nothing to really worry about,* I tried to convince myself.
>
> "Who's the president, Krickitt?"
> "Nixon."
>
> *Well, he was the president when she was born,* I justified.
>
> "Krickitt, what's your mother's name?" the therapist continued.

"Mary," she said with no hesitation . . . and no expression. *Now we're getting somewhere. Thank you, God!*

"Excellent, Krickitt. And what's your father's name?"

"Gus."

"That's right. Very good." He paused before continuing, "Krickitt, who's your husband?"

Krickitt looked at me with eyes void of expression. She looked back at the therapist without answering.

"Krickitt, who's your husband?"

Krickitt looked at me again and back at the therapist. I was sure everyone could hear my heart thudding as I waited for my wife's answer in silence and desperation.

"I'm not married."

No! God, please!

The therapist tried again. "No, Krickitt, you are married. Who's your husband?"

She wrinkled her brow. "Todd?" she questioned.

Her old boyfriend from California? Help her remember, God!

"Krickitt, please think. Who's your husband?"

"I told you. I'm not married."[64]

Because of the trauma to her brain, she had no memory of loving Kim, let alone marrying him. In fact, she had no idea who Kim Carpenter was. It would be a devastating circumstance for anyone—to be utterly forgotten by the person you love the most. But despite the difficulty, Kim—sustained by his faith in Jesus Christ—determined to win his wife's love all over again.

That is much like what God envisions in the latter part of Hosea 2, when he says,

"But I will woo her again.
>   I will take her out into the wilderness,
>   and romance her with words.
I will give her back her vineyards
>   and turn her Valley of Trouble into a Doorway
>   of Hope.
And she will respond to me as she did when she
>   was young,
>   when I brought her out of slavery in Egypt."[65]

It is also God's way with me. And with you. Despite our insensitivity and unresponsiveness, despite our moral and spiritual coma, God is determined to woo us and win us over and over again. He is the Hound of Heaven, pursuing us "with unhurrying chase, / And unperturbèd pace," as Francis Thompson depicts him in his classic poem:

I fled Him, down the nights and down the days;
>   I fled Him, down the arches of the years;
I fled Him, down the labyrinthine ways
>   Of my own mind; and in the mist of tears
I hid from Him, and under running laughter.
>   Up vistaed hopes I sped;
>   And shot, precipitated,
Adown Titanic glooms of chasmèd fears,
From those strong Feet that followed, followed after.
>   But with unhurrying chase,
>   And unperturbèd pace,
Deliberate speed, majestic instancy,
>   They beat—and a Voice beat

More instant than the Feet—
   "All things betray thee, who betrayest Me." . . .

That Voice is round me like a bursting sea:
   "And is thy earth so marred,
   Shattered in shard on shard?
Lo, all things fly thee, for thou fliest Me!
   Strange, piteous, futile thing,
Wherefore should any set thee love apart?
Seeing none but I makes much of naught," He said,
"And human love needs human meriting:
   How hast thou merited—
Of all man's clotted clay the dingiest clot?
   Alack, thou knowest not
How little worthy of any love thou art!
Whom wilt thou find to love ignoble thee
   Save Me, save only Me?
All which I took from thee I did but take,
   Not for thy harms,
But just that thou might'st seek it in my arms.
   All which thy child's mistake
Fancies as lost, I have stored for thee at home;
   Rise, clasp My hand, and come!"

Halts by me that footfall;
   Is my gloom, after all,
Shade of His hand, outstretched caressingly?
   "Ah, fondest, blindest, weakest,
I am He Whom thou seekest!
Thou dravest love from thee, who dravest Me."[66]

When I, the "strange, piteous, futile thing" of Thompson's poem, awake to the depth of my need, how unworthy I am of his love, then I may begin to feel a flicker of love flame in my heart. When I awake to the fact that the One I have ignored, neglected, and avoided is the very Love I seek—and when, instead of running from him, I rise and clasp his hand—then I have begun to fall in love with God.

Krickitt Carpenter never regained a memory of falling in love with Kim. Nor has she ever remembered marrying him. But, with the advice of a wise counselor, she and Kim started from scratch. They went on dates: bowling, ball games, golf, pizza joints, and so on. They got to know and love each other all over again. They even renewed their marriage vows in a second ceremony, two and a half years after the accident that erased Krickitt's memory.

She explained, "How can you not care deeply for somebody who has stood by you like Kimmer has stood by me? I want to remember giving my hand to him in marriage. . . . I have snapshot memories of my life just before the accident, but I don't have heart memories. . . . That's what I want."[67]

That's what I want, too. I think that's what we all want. And understanding how God has so faithfully stood by us—even when we don't thank him, think of him, or even remember him—is a key part of the process of falling in love with God.

———————— § ————————

Lord God, my faithful Lover, you have been so good to me, in spite of all my neglect and thoughtlessness. From my earliest moments of moral awareness, I have chosen my own way instead of yours. Over and over again in my life, I have wrestled the sovereign's crown from your head and tried to place it on mine. Too many times to count, I have failed to give thanks for all your care and kindness to me—worse than that, I have whined and complained like a bratty child rather than acknowledged and appreciated all your beauty and blessing.

Awaken me, God, to your constant care and generosity. Awaken me to the ways you have stood by me and the numberless times you have withheld judgment and punishment from me. Awaken me to your redemptive and constructive purposes in anything and everything I have ever seen as suffering in my life. Awaken me to my deep, fathomless need for your mercy, grace, and love. Awaken me to all the ways that I am like your wayward people and Hosea's faithless wife, that I may rise and clasp your outstretched hand. In Jesus' name, amen.

5

Seeing with
New Eyes

I love auctions. You can find some great deals for next to nothing, which really speaks to me, because I'm cheap. Not as cheap as my dad or my oldest brother; they take the cake. Literally. They take it, as long as it's free.

Anyway, I once attended an auction in Harrison, Ohio, just a few miles from my home, with my prayer partner at the time, a friend named Jim. Jim spied an ancient sewing machine he knew his wife would like. So we kind of hovered near it and chatted and watched the action, and soon we realized the auctioneer had started the bidding on the sewing machine.

Jim played it cool. He let the bidding start without him. In fact, the auctioneer had to lower his opening bid, saying, "Who'll give me two?"

Jim said, "Oh my gosh, can you believe it? It'll never go *that* cheap!"

It didn't. Somebody bid on it, and the auctioneer said, "Who'll give me three?"

After a while, he finally got that bid, so he went to three-fifty.

And that bid was much, much slower coming, so the auctioneer asked for four, then four-fifty.

Jim was in agony. "I can't believe this!" he said. He finally bid.

The auctioneer went to five. No one bid. Jim tried to play it cool, but he was clearly excited. He looked around as the auctioneer tried to get a little more for the sewing machine.

Finally, the auctioneer slammed down the gavel and said, "Sold! For four hundred and fifty dollars!"

Jim froze. He looked at me, wide-eyed. "Bob, did he—did he say—" He swallowed. "Did he say four *hundred* and fifty dollars?"

"Yeah," I said, "that's what he said."

Oh, it was tragic. I'm not sure how good you are at math, but four hundred and fifty dollars is a long way from four dollars and fifty cents. A long way.

Jim had to swallow his pride and go to the auctioneer and tell him he misunderstood. They were not terribly understanding. It was embarrassing. Humiliating. Excruciating.

And I loved every minute of it.

The book of Hosea is the Bible's story of a man who was somehow commanded by God to marry a morally bankrupt woman, a known prostitute. Talk about your awkward weddings! That one had to be reeaaally uncomfortable, something worthy of a reality TV show, wouldn't you think? But God did it to provide Hosea—and us—with a graphic, impactful, unmistakable story that would make us fall in love with God.

This story of the prophet and the prostitute, a story of heartbreak and betrayal and agony, is the story of God's love for me and for you. But it is not a story that is meant to be simply understood, the way you understand a movie or a book; if that were the case, God could have simply explained his love to Hosea. But that's not what he did. He had Hosea *experience* what God's love feels like—how far it goes, how deep, how high, how long, and how wide.

That's what we're going to try to glimpse for ourselves as we go a little deeper into Hosea's second chapter. And if, as we do that, you can feel even a little bit of what God feels for you, it will be hard for you *not* to fall deeply—or deeper—in love with him.

I Can't Make You Love Me

Everything that happens in Hosea's first chapter happens so that Hosea can identify and portray the depth of Israel's rejection (and the depth of your rejection and mine) of God. Hosea married a prostitute and watched her bear children that didn't belong to him as a reflection of how devastating it is for a loving, caring God who wants only good things for his beloved—you and me—to watch us look everywhere but to him for the love that would fill our empty hearts. And the rejection is so deep and hurts so much that God sounds just like a jilted lover in Hosea's second chapter. Because that's what he is. He says:

> "Persuade your mother, beg her—
>> for she is no wife to me,
>> and I am no longer her husband—
> that she stop whoring around,
>> and wipe away her adulterous makeup and perfume;

or I will strip her myself,
>   naked as the day she was born,
>   remove all her pretenses
>   and expose her to utter desolation and emptiness.
And I won't stop there. I will show no mercy to
>   her children,
>   because they are the children
>   of her whorish behavior.
She has brought shame on them,
>   running after her lovers
>   for the ease and the comforts they provide,
>   bread and water,
>   wool and flax, oil, and drink.
So I will block her way with a thorny hedgerow.
>   I will wall her off from her wayward paths,
so that when she heads out for a rendezvous,
>   she will fail
>   and won't even be able to find her lovers.
Then she will have to return to her husband,
>   to a time when things were better for her."[68]

I know we read these words in the previous chapter, but oh, if you've ever been betrayed, if you've ever loved someone only to have that person desert you for a new love, then maybe, *maybe* you can connect somewhat with how Israel broke God's heart—and how you and I break his heart when we "drink the rain and turn and thank the clouds."[69] Maybe you can understand how we break God's heart when we hear the Christmas story, the Easter story, the Gospel story of what the Father gave and the Son laid down and we shrug and go back to our idols. Maybe you can grasp how we break God's heart when we act like God owes us anything but the nakedness and dryness and disgrace that our sins deserve.

Some of us have trouble falling in love with God because we've never had our eyes opened to how "naked and poor, wretched and blind"[70] we are without him, before him, apart from him—or if we have, we've forgotten it.

Rather than singing with Charles Wesley,

> I have no claim on grace,
>> I have no right to plead,
> I stand before my Maker's face
>> Condemned in thought and deed,[71]

we sing with Christina Aguilera,

> I am beautiful,
> No matter what they say.[72]

Instead of saying with Paul the Apostle,

> I know that nothing good lives in me, that is, in
>> my sinful nature,[73]

We claim, in the words of the Thomas Harris book title,

> I'm OK, you're OK.

And that only breaks the heart of God, who wants only good things for his beloved—you and me. So falling in love with him involves understanding the depth of my rejection of him every time I have sinned, every time I have forgotten him, every time I choose my way instead of his, my "wisdom" instead of his, my will instead of his.

But this song is not all in a minor key, because falling in love with God also means tasting the romance God wants with us.

I Want to Know What Love Is

I don't know whether it happened this way, but I wouldn't be surprised if, as God was speaking his word to Hosea in the first half of chapter 2—saying, "she is not my wife," "I will . . . remove all her pretenses," "I will block her way with a thorny hedgerow," and, "I will wall her off from her wayward paths,"—and Hosea was writing all that stuff down. And the prophet was thinking or saying, "Yeah, God, you tell her! That's right! Give it to her! This is good stuff!"

After all, that's got to be how Hosea, a betrayed husband himself, wanted to treat his unfaithful wife, Gomer, right? Who wouldn't? Remember, she hadn't just stepped out on Hosea; she had repeatedly betrayed him and cheated on him in the worst possible ways. She had twice borne children that belonged to some other man—or men. In fact, it's quite possible that Gomer didn't even know who had fathered her second and third children. So it's not hard to imagine that Hosea might have felt at least some desire to lash out at her and make her suffer for all the rejection and shame she had made him feel.

But God's words, recorded in the latter half of Hosea 2, must have shut the prophet's mouth:

> "But I will woo her again."[74]

That had to bring Hosea up short. Just when it had sounded like God was about to give faithless Israel what she deserved—and, we may well presume, instruct Hosea to do the same to Gomer—the tone of God's words changes.

> "I will take her out into the wilderness,
>   and romance her with words."[75]

Hosea must have said, "Uh, come again?" We don't know whether God was speaking to him audibly, but if so, we may imagine the prophet shaking his head or trying to clean out his ears in order to hear better. Surely he must have heard wrong.

> "I will give her back her vineyards
>   and turn her Valley of Trouble into a Doorway
>   of Hope.
> And she will respond to me as she did when she
>   was young,
>   when I brought her out of slavery in Egypt."[76]

We may read those words and think, "How nice." We may nod, as if those sentiments are more or less par for the course—you know, God is forgiving, God is loving, and so on and so forth. But Hosea—whose relationship with Gomer had recently and intentionally mirrored God's relationship with his people—must have been thinking, "You can't be *serious*, Lord! I mean, it's all well and good to forgive and forget, but this is way beyond that. She's no good for you. She'll only hurt you again. She'll only betray me—I mean, *you*—again."

But however Hosea may have reacted, whatever the prophet may have said, God nonetheless sketched out a plan for the eventual and absolute restoration of his beloved. Because he wanted Hosea to know "how wide and long and high and deep is the love of Christ . . . this love that surpasses knowledge."[77] God wanted the record to be clear: he loves like no one else. He loved Israel beyond all reason, just the way he loves you. He loves you beyond all measure. God is *so gone for you, so in love, so head over heels* that he can't stop loving you.

In fact, the New International Version of Hosea 2:19–20 says,

> I will betroth you to me forever;
> I will betroth you in righteousness and justice,
>   in love and compassion.
> I will betroth you in faithfulness,
>   and you will acknowledge the LORD.[78]

Notice, it says,

> I will betroth you . . .
> I will betroth you . . .
> I will betroth you . . .

Not once; three times he says it, maybe because in Hebrew the typical way to express greater degrees of a quantity or a quality was not to say, for example, "more holy" or "most holy," but to say, "holy, holy, holy." Therefore, it's possible that the repetition of the word "betroth" was to impress upon Hosea—and us—how closely, how firmly, how utterly God intended to bind himself to his beloved. Or it could be that saying, "I will betroth you," three times is a reflection of God's triune nature, as though Father, Son, and Holy Spirit were all saying, "I will betroth you." Or, it's possible that the repetition was used primarily as a poetic device, stressing God's passion for his beloved, like the "I love you, I love you, I love you," of Lennon and McCartney's song "Michelle."

There is another possibility. It may be "all of the above," as God says to Hosea, and to ancient Israel, and to you, "I love you so much, I'm so gone for you, I'm so head over heels in love with you that I will bind you to me utterly and romance you forever."

Can you possibly put yourself in that story and not fall in love with a God who would look beyond your faults, your rejection, your betrayal, your indifference, your running from his love, and still love you with such an unreasonable, immeasurable, unstoppable love?

Have You Seen Her?

The poetry of Hosea's second chapter gives way, in Hosea 3, to narrative, as Hosea returns to telling what happened next:

> And Yahweh said to me, "Go and find your wife
> again, though she has betrayed you and taken up with
> another man."[79]

Now, maybe Hosea saw this coming. Maybe the incredible mercy and kindness God revealed toward his faithless beloved in chapter 2 sort of prepared the prophet for what God would say next. But even so, can you imagine?

Who would blame Hosea if he thought he was done with Gomer? Who would hold it against him if he was ready to move on with his life? Who would not sympathize if the prophet had answered God, "Come *on*! Really? *Again*? Give me a break, Lord!"

Perhaps God had to remind Hosea that his story was not just his story and that Gomer's story was not just her story. Maybe he clued the prophet in to the bigger picture. He may even have given his prophet some time to adjust to the next steps he was to take. We don't know. All we know is what Hosea recorded—probably a bare summary of the painful facts:

> And Yahweh said to me, "Go and find your wife
> again, though she has betrayed you and taken up with
> another man. Love her as I love Israel, though they have
> prostituted themselves with other gods."

> So I scraped together the slave price—though it was
> all I had—and bought her.[80]

Those few words may not seem to say much at first glance. But they say a lot. About Hosea. About God. And about you.

Can't Buy Me Love

Hosea does not say that he had to woo his wife or win back her love. He tells us that he had to buy her. He doesn't say where or from whom, but there is good reason to believe that she was being auctioned in the slave market, probably for debts she couldn't pay once Hosea, having divorced her, cut off all means of support.[81] "So I scraped together the slave price," Hosea says, "though it was all I had—and bought her."[82]

The original text says the same thing, but a little differently. The English Standard Version of the Bible is typical of how most versions translate Hosea 3:2. It says,

> I bought her for fifteen shekels of silver and a homer
> and a lethech of barley.[83]

"A homer and a lethech of barley" was a homer and a half. A homer of barley was worth around ten shekels, so a homer and a lethech of barley would have brought fifteen shekels. So Hosea paid fifteen shekels of silver plus fifteen shekels' worth of goods for his wife. My math skills aren't the best, but I'm pretty sure that means Hosea paid the equivalent of thirty shekels of silver.

Long before, when the Law was given through Moses, thirty shekels of silver had been established as the replacement price of a slave:

> If [a] bull gores a male or female slave, the owner must
> pay thirty shekels of silver to the master of the slave.[84]

So, apparently, Hosea paid the long-established slave price for his wife. And this was not a small sum of money, as indicated by the fact that Hosea paid half in cash and half in goods. He had to scrape together the means to make the purchase. It cost him dearly. It exhausted his resources. He had to sacrifice to get his bride back.

Once the thirty pieces of silver were exchanged, Hosea redeemed his bride from her life of sin, obeying God's command to "love her as I love Israel." The story continues, in verse 3, in Hosea's words:

> I told her, "You will live with me from now on. You will
> no longer be a whore. You will give yourself to no other
> man. And I will pledge the same to you."
>
> For my beloved, Israel, will be taken from me,
> and they will live many years in exile, in poverty, in
> emptiness. But they will return. They will long for me,
> and they will know what they lost. And they will be
> relieved and happy when I come to take them back.[85]

The redemption of Gomer by Hosea foreshadowed the day when, after many years of living "stripped of security and protection," as *The Message* paraphrase puts it, "without religion and comfort, godless and prayerless,"[86] the people God loves, the ones who rejected him, the ones he vowed to romance, would be ransomed and redeemed by the unreasonable, immeasurable love of their tireless Lover. It presaged the return of God's people to their homeland—and to the worship of God—after seventy years of exile in Babylon, a return that is told about in the Bible books of Nehemiah and Ezra.

It also signifies another day, when that same Lover would seek and ransom and restore me. And you. And how would he do it? With a sacrifice that cost him dearly, one that showed his love for his bride, that paid the price to redeem you and me from slavery.

He sought me

Do you remember that God told Hosea, "Go and find your wife again?"[87] Gomer didn't come to him. Hosea went to her, because God told him to. And God told him to do that because it would reflect the unreasonable, immeasurable love of our tireless Lover . . . for us. For me, and for you.

I have faint memories of a Sunday morning when I was probably no more than five or six years old. I stood from my seat among the others in our children's church and somehow ended up kneeling at an old wooden altar at the front. There, I prayed a simple prayer, confessing all my childish sins—which were many, I assure you— and asking Jesus to take up residence in my heart. It may have been the first time I sought the Lord's cleansing and saving power in my life. But it was far from the last. Still, I know that, long before I stood from that seat and long before I knelt at that altar and sought salvation, my Lover Lord sought me. He sought me even before I knew I was lost. He sought me long before I knew the truth of Paul the Apostle's words:

> I am unspiritual, sold as a slave to sin. . . . What a
> wretched man I am! Who will rescue me . . . ? Thanks
> be to God—through Jesus Christ our Lord.[88]

Jesus described a shepherd going out to find a single lost sheep and a woman turning the house upside down to find a precious heirloom to depict God's seeking concern for his beloved ones.

Similarly, in Hosea, God's love for you and me is portrayed as a broken-hearted husband who goes out looking for his unfaithful wife and finds her in a slave market.

Songwriter Sidney Cox expressed it when he wrote the chorus,

> He sought me, He sought me,
> When I was wandering far away;
> He found me, He found me,
> Oh, what a wonderful day![89]

He ransomed me

Did Hosea find Gomer in the slave market on the day she was to be auctioned off? Or did he find her and learn of her impending fate? We don't know.

Did he have to return home to scrape together the money and goods that would buy her back before someone else could buy her? Or did he have time to save up? Did he tell anyone else what he was doing? Did he face resistance from concerned family members and friends? Did Gomer ask him to do it? Did she even suspect what he was going to do ahead of time? We don't know.

We only know that Hosea, having already married Gomer and loved her as a wife, somehow found the courage and the resources to forgive her betrayals and ransom her from slavery for the slave price of thirty shekels.

It was the very price that bought Judas's betrayal and led to the arrest and crucifixion of Jesus:

> One of the Twelve, the one named Judas Iscariot, went to the cabal of high priests and said, "What will you give me if I hand him over to you?" They settled on

thirty silver pieces. He began looking for just the right moment to hand him over.[90]

Thirty silver pieces. The slave's price.

But that was not the price paid for you. Oh, no. An interesting little switcheroo took place in your case. For while it was the slave price that betrayed Jesus, your ransom was immeasurably more costly:

> For . . . it was not with perishable things such as silver or gold that you were redeemed from the empty way of life handed down to you from your forefathers, but with the precious blood of Christ, a lamb without blemish or defect.[91]

Much as he had to Hosea, the Father said to Y'shua, "Go, find Bob, though he has betrayed you and taken up with another." He said, "Go, find . . . [*you*]. Let's send them all we've got. Let's use every last resource, the brightest treasure of heaven. Love him, love her, with your body and your blood, redeem them from their slavery, from the empty way of life handed down to them from their forefathers so that I can betroth them to me forever. So that I can betroth them in righteousness and justice, in love and compassion. So that I can betroth them in faithfulness, and they can be my beloved once more, and they will say, 'You are my God.'"

And so he did. Jesus—Y'shua—the King of Heaven, the Alpha and Omega, the Sinless One, who had every right to stand aloof and let us suffer in our stubbornness and sin, instead came to earth "to give his life as a ransom for many."[92] He ransomed us with all he had . . . with his very life.

He restored me

Hosea 3:3 conveys the only recorded words the prophet spoke to his wife. Up to that point, we've read God's words and Hosea's account of his actions, but we haven't heard Hosea speak directly to his wife until:

> I told her, "You will live with me from now on. You will no longer be a whore. You will give yourself to no other man. And I will pledge the same to you."[93]

In other words, she was brought into his house, but not into his bed. Some translations phrase Hosea's words as more clearly indicating that they would also refrain from intimacy with each other:

> I said to her, "You must stay with me for many days; you won't act like a prostitute; you won't have sex with a man, nor I with you."[94]

Hosea doesn't say whether this would be a permanent or temporary arrangement, but in all likelihood it was temporary. Remember, Hosea now owned Gomer. He had purchased her. He could have done anything he liked with her, yet he prescribed a period of chastity not only for her, but also for himself.

Maybe this was a way of wiping the slate clean, of making it clear to Gomer that she had not been ransomed to be a slave, or to be used in any way. Maybe this time of abstention was designed to reset not only their relationship, but also Gomer's heart and mind as well. Especially in light of the next verses, maybe the prophet intended to wait until love and trust were rekindled between him and his beloved before intimacy also was restored. But, regardless, Gomer was restored to Hosea's home "for many days," and care was provided for her, with no strings attached.

So it is with you. God in Christ ransomed you for *you*. Not for anything he could get out of you, nor for anything you could give him or provide him, but for you. For love of you.

He waited for me

The final verses of Hosea 3 turn the story of Hosea and Gomer once again to their parallel with the story of God and his beloved, Israel—which is likewise the story of God and his beloved, the Church. So, after Hosea tells the story of ransoming Gomer from the slave market and bringing her home, God says,

> For my beloved, Israel, will be taken from me, and they
> will live many years in exile, in poverty, in emptiness.
> But they will return. They will long for me, and they
> will know what they lost. And they will be relieved
> and happy when I come to take them back.[95]

These verses refer to the impending disaster that would come on Israel, when (in 723 BC) their nation would be destroyed and their population carried into captivity by the Assyrians. But, God foresees a time when, after "many years," he would redeem them and restore them to their home. "And they will be relieved and happy when I come to take them back," he says, perhaps suggesting that Gomer was relieved and happy when Hosea appeared in the slave market to buy her and save her from a fearful fate.

We know from history, of course, that Israel—and then, in 586 BC, Judah—did indeed spend "many years" in exile before the people of God returned to their homeland. It was surely a dark and desperate period for those who lived in those days. But, through it all, God waited. He remained faithful to them, though they had been unfaithful to him. The purpose of their separation was for good, not evil. And, as he promised, his beloved longed for him and came to realize what they had lost . . . and were overwhelmed with relief and happiness when they returned.

God waited for you, too. You may not have endured years of exile in a strange land, but there have probably been periods when you were unfaithful to him and distanced yourself from him. But God waited. He ransomed you in Christ. He restored you by grace. And he waited for you to long for him and awaken to all you were missing.

———————— § ————————

Gracious God, my King, thank you for these new insights into how wide and long and high and deep is your love for me—that you would go so far to seek me, condescend so low to ransom me, open your heart wide to restore me and persevere so long to wait for me. Such knowledge is too great for me; I can't even begin to comprehend it. And yet I feel it, Lord. I feel it.

As I contemplate all your loving thoughts and actions toward me, I feel my heart strangely warmed by the entrance of your love. Please continue this work in me, and help me to draw closer and closer and fall deeper and deeper in love with you, my soul's Lover and Friend, in Jesus' name, amen.

6

Tracing
the Decline

*S*he glowed.

Her name was Roberta, and her face shone with the light of her newfound love for God. You could tell by looking at her that she was in love; she smiled, she laughed, she seemed to be full of the kind of faith that Peter says produces "joy unspeakable and full of glory."[96] No one who spent even a few moments in her presence could fail to be entranced and impressed by the light of love that filled her and shined from her.

Within the course of the next year, however, her marriage had ended, and she was preparing to enter into a second. She'd lost her glow. The light in her face was gone. She no longer worshiped in any church. She avoided her Christ-following friends and rebuffed her church's and pastor's efforts to offer comfort and counsel. The same person who just months earlier had been a glowing head-over-heels lover of God became thoroughly embittered and insensitive to him.

How does that happen?

It is rare enough to fall *in* love, right? And, sad as it is, falling in love with another human being is no guarantee that the fires of love will always burn as hot as they did at the beginning. Love sometimes cools. People often change. But people who fall in love with God can at least expect the object of their passion not to change. After all, God has said, "I the LORD do not change."[97] He "does not change like shifting shadows."[98] So how can anyone who has once experienced the wonder and beauty of falling in love with God ever fall *out* of love with him? Somehow, it happens. And when it does, it is not because God has changed. Of course not.

You Don't Bring Me Flowers

We have explored together the first three chapters of the story of Hosea, who was commanded by God to marry a prostitute in order to provide us with a graphic and impactful depiction of God's unfathomable love for us. But we're barely getting going in the journey of falling in love with God when Hosea shows us rather abruptly how terrible, ugly, and destructive it is to reject our Divine Lover's advances . . . at any stage in the romance. In chapters 4 and 5 of the book that bears his name, the prophet Hosea depicts six tragic signs of a heart that is falling out of love with God.

He says:

> Hear me now, my people, Israel,
>   for Yahweh has a grievance against you.
> "There is no faithfulness or love in you;
>   you don't even know your own husband;
> You break promises, you lie, kill,
>   steal, and commit adultery.
> You have no limits.

You go from bad to worse.
That is why you're unhappy
    and filled with anguish and regret.
Even the beasts of the field are languishing,
    and the birds are depressed.
    Not even the fish in the sea are thriving.

"And you priests can argue all you want,
    and try to blame someone else,
        but you are at fault more than anyone;
You're nothing but wayward children.
And you prophets are playing 'follow the leader'
        in disobedience,
    oblivious to the destruction of your mother, Israel.
My beloved is ruined by her cluelessness!

"You priests reject knowledge,
    so I reject you as priests.
You prophets have forgotten the Law,
    I also will forget you."[99]

Now, remember, these are the people of God he's addressing—Israel, the nation he delivered from Egypt. This is his beloved, his bride, his prized possession, who once shined with "the light of the knowledge of God's glory."[100] And yet, he says there is no awareness of God in the whole land. They are "destroyed for lack of knowledge,"[101] as the King James Version translates verse 6.

But when he says they are destroyed for lack of knowledge, he's not talking about head knowledge, though it is often misinterpreted that way. He's not talking about the kind of knowledge you exercise when you recite your ABCs or add 2 + 2. No, he's talking about the kind of knowledge you mean when you tell someone incredibly attractive and appealing to you, "I'd really like to get to *know* you."

It's the kind of knowledge he will later refer to in chapter 6 with the words,

> Oh, that we might *know* the LORD!
> Let us press on to *know* him![102]

That's what Hosea means by the "knowledge" of God. And I can tell you from my experience, when I stop pressing on to know God, when I stop spending time with him, when I neglect my relationship with him, I very quickly start to think things, feel things, and do things that I'd never do when my relationship with him is close.

That's where cursing, lying, murdering, stealing, adultery, and bloodshed come from . . . a lack of knowledge of God. A lack of closeness to him. A broken relationship with him destroys me, destroys the kind of person I want to be, destroys everything I touch, because all good things come from God and flow out of knowing him.

As with a boyfriend or girlfriend, as with a husband or wife, so it is with God: when you start to lose touch, when you make yourself a stranger to someone, you begin to lose whatever love connection you once had.

Hungry Heart

Hosea goes on, under the inspiration of the Holy Spirit, to depict the hunger of a heart that is not in love with God. He says,

> The more priests there are, the more sin there is.
> The more pride, the more shame.
> The more sins the people commit, the more sacrifices
>   they offer.

The more sacrifices, the more the priests like it.
Therefore, you are all in it together.
    As go the priests, so go the people.
    All will suffer the consequences of their actions.

"You will gorge yourselves, but never be full;
    you will whore around, but gain nothing,
because you have forsaken your Husband
    for idolatry and drunkenness,
    which make you stupid.
My beloved would rather talk to a statue,
    and listen to a stick of wood.
For she has been seduced by a spirit of whoredom,
    and has left me in order to play the whore.
Instead of worshiping me,
    my people sacrifice to idols on the mountaintops
    and give offerings on the hills;
they prostitute themselves in the shade
    of oak, poplar, and terebinth.
There, unsurprisingly, your daughters imitate your lewd
      behavior
    and your wives commit adultery.[103]

St. Augustine famously said, "O Lord . . . Thou madest us for
Thyself and our heart is restless, until it repose in Thee."[104] When
you start to make yourself a stranger to God, when you start to lose
touch with him, when you neglect prayer and the Bible and worship,
your heart will get hungrier and hungrier, and you will look under
any rock, under any tree, to the strangest things—even to a stick of
wood or a cylinder of stone, like the idols the Israelites fashioned—
to try to fill that emptiness.

In that respect, the human heart resembles the common clothes moth, which sometimes goes into a molting frenzy in its caterpillar stage if its food intake has been insufficient. Then, the caterpillar will begin molting repeatedly, changing its skin many times, and shrinking in size with every change. "The diminution process," writes Pulitzer Prize–winning author Annie Dillard, "could, in imagination, extend to infinity, as the creature frantically shrinks and shrinks and shrinks to the size of a molecule, then an electron, but never can shrink to absolute nothing and end its terrible hunger."[105]

Some people will try to end their terrible hunger with awards or parties, others with religion or hobbies, promiscuity or power. But not only will those things not fill your heart, they will do worse. In the New International Version, verse 11 reads,

> They have deserted the LORD to give themselves to prostitution, to old wine and new, which take away the understanding of my people.[106]

The Hebrew word translated "understanding" in that verse is *leb*, a word that is usually translated "heart." Those empty pursuits like promiscuity and drunkenness actually suck the heart right out of you.

If you're not finding your heart's desire in communion with God, in a closet, as Jesus put it, you won't find it. Period. Because a heart that's not head over heels in love with God is an empty heart.

You Don't See Me

Once a distance occurs in a love relationship and affection fades, the next step in the process is cloudy and confused vision, which poisons a person's decision making:

"But who can blame them
>   when their priests and prophets,
>   their fathers and husbands,
>   have led the way into depravity, ignorance, and ruin?

"How pathetic you've become, O Israel.
>   Look at her and be warned, Judah.

"Stay away from the sacred circles.
>   Steer clear of the house of idols.
>   Don't deceive yourself into thinking
>   you can mix the worship of Yawheh and idols.
Israel is a stubborn mule;
>   can I feed her like a lamb in verdant pastures?
She clings to idols;
>   let her be.
They drink themselves silly,
>   then they sin themselves stupid.
And those who should be correcting them
>   love their shameful behavior.
They are caught up in a whirlwind
>   that will end only in shame.[107]

God, the jilted Groom of Israel, laments his people's blindness. His bride has become "pathetic." His people "drink themselves silly, then they sin themselves stupid." It is a vicious, destructive cycle, a whirlwind that will end only in shame.

Isn't that always the way? Believe me, I know from experience. When I start to stray in my heart, neglect my relationship with God, make myself a stranger, and leave him standing on the dance floor while I'm sipping at the punch bowl, my vision starts to cloud and things I would have called "sin" I don't even notice anymore. I become more and more stubborn in my self-deceit, like a headstrong cow or a stubborn mule, and my gracious, loving God might well say, "Leave him alone. His vision is clouded by his sin."

And, as he does with Israel in this passage, God, my partner, must become my opponent so that my hypocrisy, stubbornness, and rebellion don't influence those around me:

> Look at her and be warned, Judah.[108]

Israel, where Hosea lived and prophesied, was one of the two kingdoms resulting from a split that occurred after the death of King Solomon. Judah was the other. God loved them both. He sent prophets to both. But Israel, the northern kingdom, managed to consistently outdo Judah in idolatry and apostasy—to such an extent that Israel's destruction would precede Judah's by several generations.

So God says to Judah, in effect, "It's more than enough that Israel betrays my love. Because of her clouded vision, she can't even see how her actions may tempt others to do the same. Don't be fooled, Judah. Look at her and be warned."

Smoke Gets in Your Eyes

Hosea's fifth chapter begins with the same word that began chapter 4: *shema*. It was the word with which all Jews of Hosea's day (and centuries before and since) began their daily prayers: "Hear." *Shema*. The first word of Deuteronomy 6:4:

> Hear, O Israel: The LORD our God, the LORD is one.[109]

So, it would have been arresting for Hosea, who probably spoke these words audibly, publicly, perhaps in the marketplace, to shout, *"Shema!"*

"Hear me now, you priests!
    Pay close attention, Israel!
Mark my words, royal family!
    I will put this as clearly as possible:
You have been an evil influence at Mizpah
    and led the people astray at Tabor.
You have descended deep into sin, all of you,
    so I will go to great lengths to correct you.
I know you intimately;
    I still see you clearly,
though you are covered in whoredom,
    you are defiled by your unfaithfulness.

"You are ensnared in your own sin;
    your pride and stubbornness hold you back from
        returning to me.
Your whoring ways have blinded you,
    so that you no longer even recognize my face.[110]

A heart that turns away from God, a declining relationship with him, an empty heart, and a clouded vision can result in nothing *but* corrupt actions.

There is no one righteous, not even one.[111]

Apart from God, no one can produce a pure life. Jesus said,

Apart from me you can do nothing.[112]

Hosea 5:4 says:

You are ensnared in your own sin;

your pride and stubbornness hold you back from
returning to me.[113]

The New International Version renders that verse,

> Their deeds *do not permit them* to return to their
> God.[114]

Do you see how accurate that is? I would be hard pressed to count how many times I've sat, as a pastor, with someone who is empty hearted—*and knows it*—yet claims that they can't return to their God because "that would mean moving out of my girlfriend's house" or "that would mean shutting down my business" or "that would mean letting him win." Their deeds *do not permit them* to return to their God.

Not long ago, television's History Channel produced a highly acclaimed, much-watched miniseries called *Hatfields & McCoys*, about the famous family feud that spanned decades and stained red with blood the border between Kentucky and West Virginia. It is a true and tragic story, one that my wife and I watched together. As the story unfolded, we were repeatedly struck by how just one small conciliatory move at any number of points along the murderous trail could have stopped the bloodshed and saved numerous lives. But pride and stubbornness prevented them.

So it was with Israel. And so, very often, is it with us. "I could *never* go back now," we say. What we mean, of course, is that our pride prevents us. Or our stubbornness. Or some other sinful attitude. And, unavoidably, our actions become more and more corrupt, and we become more and more trapped by our repeated betrayal of God's love for us.

And the results of such a course can be nothing but tragic.

Look What You've Done to Me

A declining relationship with God, an empty heart, a clouded vision, and the resulting corrupt actions lead inevitably to tragic consequences, as Hosea warns in chapter 5, verses 8–11:

> "Sound the alarm now,
>> for your destruction is coming:
> Certain,
>> unavoidable,
>> and extreme.
> Your leaders are crooked and corrupt,
>> and I will no longer hold back the punishment
>>> they deserve.
>> I will let loose on them.
> I will cast you to the gutter
>> since you were so determined to go there.[115]

In those verses, God is vividly warning Israel through Hosea that their separation from him, their rejection of his unfathomable love, will result in tragic consequences. In the English Standard Version, verse eight reads:

> Blow the horn in Gibeah,
>> the trumpet in Ramah.
> Sound the alarm at Beth-aven;
>> we follow you, O Benjamin![116]

Gibeah, Ramah, and Beth Aven were border towns, just across the border from Israel into Judah (or Benjamin, as the southern kingdom was also called). The idea is of a general alarm announcing impending destruction. It's a little like hearing civil defense sirens

Falling in Love with God

sounding in Detroit; you know the Canadians are going to invade any minute!

That's what God is saying to his beloved: "your rejection of my tender love is going to have tragic consequences for you: you'll be laid waste—Judah, too, in due time, but Israel first."

That is always the way. When my connection with God begins to decline, when I begin to treat him like a stranger instead of the Lover of my soul, tragic consequences are inevitable. It is only by God's mercy that I'm not consumed already, burned to a crisp long ago by the consequences of my own willful, corrupt actions. And if I don't "nip it in the bud," so to speak, when the fervor of my relationship with God begins to wane, I'll experience the final symptom of a heart that has fallen out of love with God.

Total Eclipse of the Heart

The last four verses of Hosea 5 are awful, horrible words to read. God tells those he loves that the path they are on leads nowhere but to total devastation.

> I will chew you up like a moth,
> > and will let your sins eat at you like dry rot.
>
> "When you, Israel, woke up to your own sickness,
> > and Judah became aware of his condition,
> you sent to Assyria for help,
> > and appealed to that despot!
> But he can't help you.
> > He will only make matters worse.
> All my tenderness toward you has gotten me nowhere,
> > so I will turn it off completely.
> I will rip and shred you like a lion,

94

> I will tear you to pieces like a grizzly.
> Then I will return to my hiding place,
>> until you have learned your lesson,
> And come to your senses,
>> and come looking for me . . ."[117]

"I have chewed you up like a moth," God says, "and have let your sins eat at you like dry rot." In other words, like a moth destroying fabric or dry rot ravaging wood, he has been letting his beloved suffer the slow, destructive consequences of her actions.

But in verse 13, God says that Israel, once she saw the terrible consequences of her betrayal of God's love—instead of turning to him and loving him again—turned to Tiglath-Pileser, the "great king" of Assyria, expecting *him* to deliver her.

So he says, "I will be like a lion." No more gradual. No more slow. Suddenly, he will let her experience total desperation.

How cruel, right?

No. Not at all. Because God's object is, as he states in the last verse of Hosea 5, for her to learn her lesson, come to her senses, and once again come looking for him.

"Behold therefore the goodness and severity of God,"[118] as Romans 11:22 says. He will tear us to pieces, he will wound us, he will let us experience the tragic consequences of our sinful ways. But his purpose in doing so is that, when we reach the end of our rope, we will reach out and find him there.

———————— § ————————

Lord God, Lover of my soul, you have done so much for me. You have made known to me the path of life and filled me with joy in your presence (Ps. 16:11). Yet, I confess that I am prone to wander, prone to leave the God I love. Please have mercy on my feeble and fickle heart, and help me to be properly warned by your Word. Help me not to tolerate even the slightest distance from you and, if I do wander, to turn quickly back to you, the source of all my blessing and joy. Make me and keep me wholly and always devoted to you. In Jesus' name, amen.

Grasping the
Lover's Desire

It seemed like a match made in heaven.

She was a beauty queen whose Hollywood star had finally risen. Her movie roles included that of Kathy Selden in the 1952 hit *Singin' in the Rain*, with Gene Kelly and Donald O'Connor. She had even scored a hit record in 1951 with the song "Aba Daba Honeymoon" from the 1950 film *Two Weeks with Love*.

He was one of the most popular singers in the world, having scored twenty-four songs in the Top Ten on the music charts between 1950 and 1955, including number one hits "Wish You Were Here," "I'm Walking behind You," "I Need You Now," and the international chart-topper, "Oh! My Pa-Pa."

In 1955, Debbie Reynolds and Eddie Fisher were married. The next year, they costarred in the musical comedy *Bundle of Joy*. That same year (1956), they welcomed their first child into the world—Carrie (who later became an actress herself). In 1957, Debbie Reynolds's song "Tammy" became a number one hit, and the next year, their son Todd was born. They were the "It" couple before there was such a term. They "seemed to seep fairy-tale bliss from their pores,"[119] as one writer put it. They were famous, successful, and beloved.

Then it ended. In March 1958, movie producer Mike Todd—a close friend of Eddie Fisher—died in a plane crash. Todd was also the husband of Debbie Reynolds's best friend: the famous and beautiful film star Elizabeth Taylor. Reportedly, Fisher tried to console Taylor, and eventually the two started an affair. Reynolds discovered the affair by accident, as she recounted a few years ago to a journalist:

> Lonely at home, while Eddie was away on tour, she telephoned her best friend Elizabeth Taylor at her hotel for a chat.
>
> To her great shock, Fisher answered.
>
> "Suddenly, a lot of things clicked into place," she recalls. "I could hear her voice asking him who was calling—they were obviously in bed together. I yelled at him, 'Roll over, darling and let me speak to Elizabeth.'"
>
> Fisher slammed the receiver down and rushed home for a face-to-face confrontation. "I'm sorry," he told her. "Elizabeth and I are in love and I want a divorce."[120]

So sudden. So tragic. So heartless.

It was a seismic Hollywood scandal, far more shocking than the celebrity scandals of our day, which are so frequent and common they hardly surprise anyone anymore. But the Debbie Reynolds/ Eddie Fisher/Elizabeth Taylor triangle was a big deal in its day. It won widespread sympathy for Reynolds, who went on to even greater success, and largely scuttled Fisher's career. And it provides a more contemporary background to the situation described in

Hosea—not only between Hosea and his wife Gomer, but also between God and his people Israel.

Can you imagine? How horrible it would feel to call a friend in a moment of loneliness for your beloved and suddenly discover that friend in bed with your beloved. It would change so much. It would hurt so badly. And it would be something like what God and his prophet endured in the days of Hosea.

You Don't Fool Me

At the end of Hosea 5, God said he would let Israel suffer. He told them he would rip and shred and tear them to pieces, and then, like a lion or bear, head into his den where they would have trouble finding him. Then, he foresaw, they would come looking for him, saying,

> "Come, let us return to Yahweh;
>> for he has hurt us that he may heal us;
>> he has wounded that he may make us whole.
> In short order, he will restore us;
>> on the third day he will raise us up to a brand new
>>> life with him.
> Let us find him again; let us get to know him once more.
>> Surely he will greet us like the dawn;
> He will refresh us
>> as he sends rain on the earth after a cold, hard winter."[121]

Let's put this into perspective. Israel had been doing some pretty horrible things during this time, things that not only hurt God but also displayed their willingness—even eagerness—to hurt him. He says, in Hosea 6:7–11:

> "But like your first parents you have rejected me
>> and walked out on me.

You have turned places of refuge into crime scenes,
>   and priests into robbers!
Nothing is sacred to you;
>   everything you touch becomes vile.
I don't even recognize my beloved anymore;
>   I see only a whore,
>   only filth when I look at you.

"And you, Judah, are no better.

"Your fate will be no different."[122]

God is letting them know, "You may *say,* 'Let us return' but you *mean,* 'He doesn't see what we do, so we'll *act* like we'll return.'" He knew where their hearts were. He knew what their words were worth. As moving and sincere as the words of Hosea 6:1–3 were— they've been made into beautiful songs over the years—God wanted them to know that he saw beyond appearances. As he said to the prophet Samuel, "People judge by outward appearance, but the LORD looks at the heart."[123]

He foresaw that showering his tough love on his beloved would prompt a show of repentance. They would say, "Let us return," but their returning would be halfhearted at best, producing no "fruit in keeping with repentance."[124]

They were like the people of Jesus' day, whom he addressed, quoting Isaiah,

> Isaiah was right when he prophesied about you
> hypocrites; as it is written:
> "These people honor me with their lips, but their
> hearts are far from me."[125]

It is so easy to go halfway with God, to think he'll be pleased with whatever scraps we give him. We draw near to him according to our needs, according to our moods. We speak lovingly to him in church and give him a cold shoulder at other times. We say the right things but produce no fruits of repentance.

We think he should be satisfied with our Sunday sainthood. We expect him to be pleased with our goose bumps at concerts and our graces at meals. But what lover would be satisfied with that? What lover is gratified by empty words and occasional attentions? What lover wants half a heart?

I Want You to Want Me

God says to his beloved Israel in verses 4–6 of Hosea's sixth chapter:

> "What am I supposed to do with you, Israel?
>> How can I get through to you, Judah?
> Your love is like morning fog,
>> like dew that disappears at daybreak.
> Can you blame me for the harsh messages my
>> prophets speak?
> Can you really fail to be moved by my cutting words,
>> my drastic actions?
> I want your faithful love, not your religious shows.
>> I want you to want me, not just my favor."[126]

Do you hear the lover's frustration in verse 4? "What am I supposed to do with you?"

How many parents have felt or said something like that to a child who is utterly loved, when they've loved and loved, tried and tried, and still gotten nowhere? "What am I supposed to do with you?" The phrase expresses God's frustration with his people.

Having suffered so much rejection and betrayal, he lets them hear his desperation.

These verses (like the whole Bible) make it clear that God is not some unfeeling force. Nor is he some distant despot who wants only tribute and obeisance; he is a Lover who desires love from his beloved. From us. From you. Like any lover, he desires to be desired. He wants to be wanted. He loves to be loved. He longs to be longed for.

He has ever and always wanted this. It is the very thing he asked for—commanded, even—from his people in the first days of the nation of Israel:

> Hear, O Israel: The LORD our God, the LORD is one.
> Love the LORD your God with all your hearts and
> with all your soul and with all your strength. These
> commandments that I give you today are to be upon
> your hearts.[127]

"I want your faithful love," he told Israel through Hosea, "not your religious shows. I want you to want *me*, not just my favor." Every lover wants that. What good are flowers or candy to a lover who feels ignored or neglected? Who would not be disappointed when a lover gives the impression—repeatedly—that the real attraction is not the lover himself or herself, but the lover's money or gifts or favors?

Some settle for that, of course. There are dating websites that list "sugar daddies," wealthy men who are being sought because they are successful, wealthy, and available. A respondent to one of these sites wrote,

> When we met I had just claimed bankruptcy on my
> home and was in such a mess. My fiancée helped pull
> me out of my mess and has loved and cherished me.

On my 25th birthday he bought me a beautiful Lexus.
And he is building me a barn for my horses (I am a
major equestrian). Everywhere we go we are treated
like celebrities. Going from struggling check to check
to now being spoiled everyday! My Sugar daddy still
buys me presents and flowers and always makes sure
my checking account has money.[128]

Another satisfied customer of the same site wrote of her "sugar daddy,"

He has taken me to the Bahamas, Paris (where we
stayed in a castle!!!!!), England, St. Barths, Malibu,
NYC ... and more![129]

In neither case is there any mention of the "sugar daddy's" personality or character (other than his generosity, of course). It seems clear that each is valued primarily for his gifts and favors. And that seems to suit some just fine.

But not God. God is love. He knows what love—true love—is, and he will settle for nothing less from his people. From me. Or you.

Bring Me All Your Lovin'

It is not just any kind of love God is intent on receiving from you. Not in quality, nor in degree. When God says in verse 6, "I want your faithful love" he uses the Hebrew word *chesed* (or *hesed*, as it is sometimes spelled). It is the same word used in verse 4, "Your love is like morning fog." Briscoe discusses the word in his book *Taking God Seriously*:

It is translated many different ways in the Old
Testament. Some people say it is related to the idea

of the covenant, therefore it has the idea of loyalty. Others say it suggests we become involved in a covenant because we have a prior love that makes us want to enter that covenant, so the idea of *hesed* is steadfast love. Other people say this loyal love demonstrates itself in kindness and generosity and mercy, and in many instances you will find the word *hesed* translated as all these different words. One word used in the older translations probably capsulizes the whole meaning: *loving-kindness.* What God says is this: When he makes a covenant with his people, it is a covenant of loyalty, love, kindness, and tender mercies which he expects to be reciprocated.[130]

God wants *chesed* from his people. He wants loyalty, love, kindness, and tender mercies. He wants the kind of love that comes out in actions, in obedience, not just in words.

He craves *your chesed*. He wants you to love him supremely and completely, with all of your heart, soul, mind, and strength—with your affections *and* actions. He desires a love from you like that of Howell Harris, a leader of the Welsh Methodist revival, who wrote, "I must have the Savior indeed, for he is my All. All that others have in the world and in religion and in themselves I have in thee—pleasures, riches, safety, honor, life, righteousness, holiness, wisdom, bliss, joy, gaiety and happiness."[131]

In fact, inspired by God, Hosea applies four metaphors to Israel that further identify and amplify the response God wants from you, today and every day. From those metaphors, each of us can chart our course if we truly want to fall in love with God.

I will redirect my passions

Hosea's seventh chapter begins:

> "Don't you see? I have wanted nothing but to love and
> heal Israel,
>   but their sins have prevented me.
> They cheat and lie,
>   they steal and rob each other.
> They think I don't see them,
>   or assume that I will look the other way.
> But they pile up sin upon sin;
>   how can I miss it?
>
> "Their evil behavior delights their king,
>   and their officials laugh at their immorality.
> Every one of them is an adulterer;
>   they are like ovens that never cool, even when empty.
> The king throws a party
>   and the princes drink until they are sick
>   and debase themselves with mockers.
> Their hearts are ovens of treachery;
>   their hatred smolders through the night
>   and blazes into flame with the morning.
> The fires of their rage consume their leaders;
>   they drop like moths in a flame.
>   None of them calls to me."[132]

God had already described Israel's love, in chapter 6, as "like morning fog," meaning it comes and goes. In the verses above, he uses a new image to communicate a similar point. He says they are "like ovens that never cool, even when empty." He is not talking about spiritual passion; he is describing their unfaithfulness to him, which shows itself in sexual immorality and debauchery.

The Swiss reformer John Calvin, in his fascinating commentary on Hosea, points out three facets of the metaphor God employs:

1. "The people were not corrupted by some outward impulse, but by their own inclination and propensity of mind; yea, by a mad and furious desire of acting wickedly."

2. This had not been the result of a sudden impulse—a mistake, perhaps, or a moment of weakness—but "the people of Israel had not only been prone to defection, but had also greedily desired it."

3. "This fire had not been suddenly lighted up, but had been for a long time gathering strength."[133]

Israel's unfaithfulness was not a momentary weakness but a lifestyle choice—and the result of many previous, smaller choices. So, it is with the heart that "falls out of love" with God. There is nothing mysterious about it. We do not suddenly find that our passions have cooled toward God; rather, we make a series of decisions that, step by step, lead us one direction or another.

The lover becomes too busy for the beloved, who begins calling less frequently, who refocuses his or her attention on the television or Internet, is taking steps away from passion, away from *chesed*. So it is in our relationship with God. If we are not as passionate about God as we were at the start, we must refocus our passions and begin to "recover your dear early love."[134]

My wife and I have observed a weekly "date night" for many years. We both reserve the time and look forward to it. We go out to eat, see movies, take hikes, attend live theater, go on scenic drives, take tours, attend concerts—almost anything that will relax us and reinvigorate our love for each other. From time to time, however, one or the other of us will begin to "cheat" the parameters of date night, by working late or asking to be excused for some reason. An occasional cancellation or rescheduling is unavoidable, of course; but when one of us begins to sense that the other is making date night less of a priority, we are quick to speak up. Our dates are one of the ways we connect with each other and keep the passion alive.

We all need something like that from time to time in our relationship with God. General William Booth, who with his wife founded The Salvation Army, once said, "It is the nature of a fire to go out; you must keep it stirred and fed and the ashes removed."[135] We must redirect our passions, rekindle the fire of our love for God ... or we are taking steps in the opposite direction.

I will renew my commitment

God continues, through his prophet, to shine a light on his people's behavior as a way of giving them a chance to wake up and turn around. He says,

> "My people try to have it both ways;
>> they are half-baked.
> Godless people sap their strength,
>> and they don't even see it;
> they're growing old before their time,
>> yet they don't see what they're doing to themselves.
> Their arrogance is so obvious,
>> yet they are blinded by it;
>> it prevents them from returning to Yahweh, despite
>> everything."[136]

"My people . . . are half-baked," God says. The King James Version renders the metaphor as, "a cake not turned." The New International Version has it, "a flat cake not turned over." The idea is the same.

The staple of daily life in Bible lands, in Hosea's day and in ours, is a flat, round loaf or cake of bread that Westerners might call a "pita pocket." It can be baked in an oven or on hot coals. The "pocket" (created by steam in the baking process) can be stuffed with meat, tomatoes, cucumbers, falafel, etc. It is easily torn into pieces that are then used to scoop sauces or dips, such as hummus. This thin type of bread must, of course, be turned over in the baking process or one side will become burned while the other side is uncooked.

Many people today are, likewise, not cooked through. Passionate one moment, apathetic the next. Half-baked in their commitment to God. Half-hearted. Trying to have it both ways. Their feet firmly planted on both sides of the fence.

The problem with half-hearted commitment is that it does no one any good. You might think that "half a loaf," so to speak, is better than no loaf. But the metaphor of the half-baked pita makes it clear: both sides suffer. I do myself no good, I do God no good, I do no one any good by straddling the fence.

At this writing, my wife and I have just celebrated our thirty-fifth anniversary. Like any couple, we have had good times and not-so-good times in our marriage, but we have only grown closer and more in love, year by year. So, a week before our anniversary, I surprised her with a renewal-of-vows ceremony on our family vacation in Tennessee with our kids and their families. Our small party drove together to the Trillium Gap trailhead in the Great Smoky Mountains National Park, then hiked the 1.2 miles to the Grotto Falls. Standing behind the twenty-five-foot high waterfall, we held each other's hands and once more committed ourselves unreservedly and irrevocably to each other.

What would it look like for you to renew your vows to God? God will not accept a half-hearted love. He is not impressed by half-baked commitments. He wants what he has always wanted: you. And *all* of you.

A favorite prayer chorus of mine never fails to draw me "behind the waterfall" with God. It is a prayer of the Salvationist songwriter Will Brand:

> By the love that never ceased to hold me,
> By the blood which Thou didst shed for me,
> Whilst Thy presence and Thy power enfold me,
> I renew my covenant with Thee.[137]

I will refocus my energies

The next metaphor God uses to describe his beloved's behavior begins in the eleventh verse:

> "My Israel is a silly bird,
>   confused and fickle,
>   flitting to Egypt for help, flying off to Assyria.
> I will toss my net
>   and trap them like the flighty creatures they are.
>   I will teach them, one way or the other.
> I will make them sorry for their waywardness.
>   I will inflict pain on them!
> I would have liked to be kind to them,
>   but they won't stop lying to me.

I would prefer for them to ask me for help,
  but they prefer to be miserable;
they cut themselves and appeal to idols,
  and turn away from me.
I am the one who cared for them and trained them,
  but they act like I'm their enemy."[138]

God likened his people to "a silly bird." In Hosea's day, Israel had sought protection from each of the two "superpowers" of the day: Egypt and Assyria. The land of Israel lay between these two powers, and, when one threatened, Israel appealed to the other for help, back and forth, trying to play one against the other, while neither was a true friend or ally. All the while, of course, God longed for them to look to *him* and rely on *him*.

I do much the same. God wants me to rely on him for my security, but I look to my checking account balance for security. God wants me to rely on him for approval, but I look to my peers. God wants me to rely on him for comfort, but I seek it in food. God wants me to rely on him for a sense of identity and respect, but I try to find it in purchases and possessions. As a result, I'm like a silly bird, confused and fickle, regularly changing plans, changing direction, changing masters.

I need to refocus my energies. I need to stop trying to slake my thirsty soul from "broken cisterns that can hold no water" and pursue instead the "fountain of living waters,"[139] the only one who will satisfy my soul. I need to plug my ears to the siren calls of this culture and this generation and focus on the one thing that is necessary, as Jesus identified it in Mary the sister of Lazarus[140]—a rapt, personal focus on God.

I will return to my first love

In Hosea's seventh chapter, God uses a domestic metaphor (ovens that never cool), a culinary metaphor (a half-baked pita), and a wildlife metaphor (silly birds). The fourth metaphor he employs to describe his beloved Israel is a military image, found in Hosea 7:16:

> "They are willing to try anything;
> > they will turn to anyone except me!
> They are like a warped bow;
> > they can't shoot straight to save their life!
> Their leaders will get what they deserve,
> > and those they've tried to impress will laugh at them."[141]

God says his people are "a warped bow." The *Moffatt* version says, "They are like a bow that swerves."[142] Other versions render it, "a treacherous bow" or "a deceitful bow." The image is of a bow, like those used in battle, that is out of whack. If it was ever "in whack."

An arrow shot from a crooked bow, of course, will not hit the target. It is unreliable and ineffective. If I am a warped bow, if I'm not in love with God and enjoying a reciprocating love relationship with him, I will miss the mark every time. All my efforts will amount to nothing. All my joys will be fleeting at best.

The human heart—the human life—is only plumb when it is centered on God. "Plumb" is a carpentry term. It refers to a line that is exactly vertical, or precisely perpendicular to a horizontal plane. In other words, if something is plumb, it is "in whack." It is true. It is straight. It is upright.

The way to return my heart and life to plumb is to reclaim my first love, as Jesus urged the church at Laodicea:

> Remember the height from which you have fallen!
> Repent and do the things you did at first.[143]

What will that look like for you? Ask God. Ask him to open your eyes to the height from which you've fallen. Ask him to turn your heart to him. Ask him to help you restore your habits and routines, the things you did when you first experienced his love. Ask him to show you what it means to truly and fully love him. Ask him to reveal himself to you in his Word. Ask him to meet you in times of prayer and enliven them and lengthen them by his overwhelming presence. Ask him to bring people into your life who will show you what it means to love him and be loved by him. Ask him to answer the following prayer in you:

———————— § ————————

Beautiful Lord God, you have always wanted only to love and heal me, but my waywardness has often prevented you, I know. Oh, Lord, save me from being like an oven that never cools, even when empty; deliver me from habits and patterns that would stoke the fires of unfaithfulness in my heart. Save me from being half baked and halfhearted; help me to renew and fulfill a wholehearted covenant with you. Save me from being like a silly bird, flitting here and there, looking for satisfaction from things that will never satisfy; help me to seek and find my soul's satisfaction in you, and only you. Save me from being like a warped bow; straighten my heart and mind and life until it is all plumb and pointed ever and always to you. Turn me away from everything that would turn me away from you. In Jesus' name, amen.

8

Relearning What
Love Is

I've been a *Nat King* Cole fan almost my whole life.

Nat King Cole was the jazz pianist and popular recording artist of the 1940s, '50s, and early '60s. He recorded such hits as "Unforgettable," "Mona Lisa," and "The Christmas Song." My mother, a talented musician in her own right, was a fan, and I inherited a collection of Nat King Cole records—and an appreciation for his smooth vocal style—from her.

When my wife, the lovely Robin, and I were training for ministry, we would make frequent trips into New York City for ministry purposes. On the way into the city, on a bus filled with our fellow students, I would sometimes serenade Robin from my vast repertoire of Nat King Cole songs.

Occasionally, I would launch the first verse of one of Nat King Cole's songs: "I just found joy, I'm as happy as a baby boy with another brand new choo-choo toy. . . ." Then, as she gazed lovingly into my eyes, I would complete the verse, "Since I met my sweet Lorraine, Lorraine, Lo . . . rraine."

She fell for it every time. But, as you might guess, she was less than appreciative once I got to the name, "Lorraine." It kinda spoiled the moment, since her name is not Lorraine. She would laugh with me, but that particular song didn't exactly stoke the fires of romance.

A lot of songs (as well as movies, television shows, and books) send wrong—or at least confusing—messages these days. Songs like "Torn between Two Lovers" and "If Loving You Is Wrong (I Don't Wanna Be Right)" sympathetically portray illicit "love" affairs. Nearly every movie and television series depicts love as roughly synonymous with casual sexual relations. And books like *Fifty Shades of Grey* confuse love with sexual experimentation and abuse.

Some of us learned about falling in love as children, perhaps from Disney movies ("Someday My Prince Will Come"), fairy tales, or parents' examples. Others of us learned about love and romance later in life—from literature, perhaps, or locker rooms. Unfortunately, much of what we "know" on the subject just ain't so.

Many of the things we have learned on the subject of love actually hinder our ability to fall in love—and stay in love with God. Much of our "knowledge" must be unlearned if we are ever going to fall in love with God.

Relearn Love

Israel was in the same predicament. They clearly had warped ideas about loving God. And a large portion of Hosea's fourteen chapters is devoted to disabusing Israel of their many mistaken notions about love, God, and their relationship with him.

But the book of Hosea was probably (almost certainly, in fact) not written all at once. "Without any doubt," wrote British evangelist, preacher, and author G. Campbell Morgan, the book of Hosea

is the prophet's own "condensation of the burden of his preaching" over a period of seventy years.[144] So it shouldn't surprise us that
Hosea keeps returning to many of the same themes and repeatedly
says many of the same things.

Even so, there is something new and fresh to be discovered in
each chapter. And chapters 8–10 of Hosea's prophecy can be understood as charting some of the twisted and wrongheaded ways Israel
(and us with them) had come to view love in general and love for
God in particular. In fact, we may well see in these three chapters
of Hosea's prophecy as many as ten symptoms of misguided ideas
about love, which in turn make it difficult to fall in love—and stay
in love—with God.

I am misled by feelings

Throughout the book of Hosea, God paints the picture of a people
who confuse love and infatuation, love and romance, love and lust.
And that was the beginning of their troubles, as it is the beginning
of ours. We inhabit a culture where people tend to make the mistake of relying exclusively on feelings, infatuation, even ecstasy, as
a measurement of love. They say things like, "I fell in love," "It was
love at first sight," and "I fell out of love."

But those concepts are not found in the Bible. They are not a
reflection of true love, and certainly not the whole story when it
comes to God's love.

Yes, God is a feeling being, though certainly there are differences between divine emotions and our emotions. But love—as
God expresses it for us and as he desires it from us—is a function of
both emotion and will, of feeling and action.

We tend to act loving only when we feel loving, only when we're
"in the mood." We think of love in terms like those sung about by

Blue Swede (and B. J. Thomas and many others): "I'm hooked on a feeling." But that is not a biblical concept of love. The Bible says,

> Love is patient, love is kind. It does not envy, it does
> not boast, it is not proud. It does not dishonor others,
> it is not self-seeking, it is not easily angered, it keeps
> no record of wrongs. Love does not delight in evil
> but rejoices with the truth. It always protects, always
> trusts, always hopes, always perseveres.[145]

Notice what those verses *don't* say. They don't say, "Love feels all warm and gooey." They don't say, "Love makes you feel lighter than air." Those things are sometimes true, but they are not the soul and substance of love, contrary to the way popular culture depicts it.

If I allow myself to be misled by feelings in my relationship with God, I should not be surprised if I end up where Israel did, as described in Hosea 8:1:

> "Get ready to sound the alarm!
> The vultures are circling, ready to prey on my people,
>   for they have rejected my love
>   and rebelled against my law."[146]

If I rely on my feelings, I will be misled. Feelings come and go. They are the result of many influences: caffeine, vitamin deficiencies, weather, traffic, and the like. If I equate love with feelings of love, then I will be tempted—and perhaps feel justified—to wane or wander when my emotions ebb.

I take God's love for granted

If I sat you down at a desk like a third grader and told you to write down every single piece of evidence in your life that God loves you, what would you write? Chances are, you would fill a sheet of note-book paper, at least. Right? You might list things like sunrises and sunsets, my healing from cancer, my children, salvation, summer, naps, my church, the flowers in my garden, and so on. You might include thunderstorms or tomatoes. If you're anything like me, Krispy Kreme donuts would be high on the list.

But, of course, most of those things are things we generally take for granted in our lives, aren't they? They seldom earn much of our attention. They're just there. As are so many more means of God's love toward us.

He defends us from numerous enemies. He fills us with joy. He is a Father to the fatherless. He is a Defender of widows. He sur-rounds us with family. He sets us free. He sends rain on our fields and gardens. He provides for our needs. He carries us in his arms like the gentle Shepherd that he is. He rescues us from death. He gives power and strength to us.[147]

Yet we even take for granted his love and all his loving actions toward us. We treat him as Israel did, as described in Hosea 8:2–3:

> "They never hesitate to say,
>> 'God, help us out. Give us a hand!'
> But they have slapped away my hand once too often;
>> now let their enemies go after them."[148]

How often has that been true of me? Of you? How often have I called out to God, asking him for this or that, and yet in almost the next breath (or with my next step), slapped away his hand? How often have I begged for help when I'm in need and then, soon after being delivered or carried through, begun acting again as though I didn't need him?

That is taking his love for granted. I do it in multiple ways. *Countless* ways.

I scatter seeds of rebellion

Hosea's next words may, at first glance, seem easy to read without applying them to ourselves:

> "They choose their own poison;
>> installing kings without thought of me,
>> crowning princes all on their own.
> With silver and gold they make idols,
>> fashioning their own destruction.
> I reject your golden calf, O Samaria.
>> It incites my anger.
> How long will you be so devoid of conscience?
> It is a toy! You made it yourself!
>> How can you worship it as a god?
>
> "You know the crop is always greater than the seed;
>> sow the wind, and you will reap a whirlwind.
> The things you are doing are empty and useless;
>> like wheat with no head, it will produce nothing.
> What little it may yield will not be worth harvesting.[149]

See what I mean? He mentions "installing kings without thought of me." And making idols out of silver and gold. He even refers to a golden calf they worshiped. You and I don't do that. Right?

Not so fast, cowpoke. Their rebellion may look as though it has nothing to do with your life and mine. But "the crop is always greater than the seed," he says. Israel was reaping the product of many tiny seeds of rebellion they had sown.

Soon after the death of King Solomon, the nation of Israel split into two kingdoms: Judah and Israel. Judah's capital—and the Temple of God—remained in Jerusalem, ruled by King Rehoboam, Solomon's son. That presented Israel—and Jeroboam—with a new problem:

> Jeroboam thought to himself, "The kingdom will now likely revert to the house of David. If these people go up to offer sacrifices at the temple of the LORD in Jerusalem, they will again give their allegiance to their lord, Rehoboam king of Judah. They will kill me and return to King Rehoboam."
>
> After seeking advice, the king made two golden calves. He said to the people, "It is too much for you to go up to Jerusalem. Here are your gods, Israel, who brought you up out of Egypt." One he set up in Bethel, and the other in Dan.[150]

It made sense. It was convenient. It saved the people a lot of time and trouble. Which is often how these things start.

I sow seeds of rebellion all the time. Not all of them sprout. Not all of them produce a crop. But they all possess the potential for a crop, and a harvest.

What are they? Chances are, they are different in your life than in mine. But they almost always begin with the pursuit of convenience. The cutting of corners. The taking of shortcuts that "God won't mind" and others won't notice. But they are all seeds, and seeds will bear a crop. And the crop is always greater than the seed.

I treat God's goodness like affliction

At the time of this writing, I have four wonderful grandchildren. Two of them, Calleigh and Ryder, who are brother and sister, were born with cystic fibrosis (CF). Cystic fibrosis is a genetic disease that causes thick mucus to accumulate in the lungs, digestive tract, and other areas of the body. It also limits the ability of a person to digest and metabolize foods properly, so a person with CF must take synthetic enzymes with every meal, to aid the digestive process.

Part of the protocol for Calleigh and Ryder's care is the ingestion of roughly 50 percent more calories every day than other children consume. This means that their parents are regularly urging—sometimes begging—them to eat potato chips, hot dogs, cupcakes, cookies, donuts, and ice cream. Can you imagine? Instead of "finish your vegetables, Junior, or there will be no cake for you," it's "you've eaten enough broccoli, please eat another cupcake, sweetie!" Many people (including me) would think they were in heaven to have Mom and Dad begging them to eat, eat, eat.

But two-year-old Calleigh is not one of those people (Ryder hasn't yet begun to eat solid food). She routinely chooses peas or protein over all those other foods. I have witnessed (and participated in) herculean battles of the will in which Calleigh's parents place all sorts of rich, sweet, and delicious foods in front of her, and yet she refuses to eat a bite. In fact, the prospect sometimes makes her cry. She sees the pressure to eat those delectable treats as afflictions.

That's a little like the way I react to the riches God sets before me, some of which resembles Israel's conduct, as described in Hosea 8:8–14:

"Do you not see? Israel is being eaten alive;
> they're already known among the nations as
>> has-beens.
They are like a donkey in heat,
> trotting off to Assyria,
> looking for love.
They have sold themselves to this lover and that lover,
> but that will soon end.
They will be dominated by one lover,
> and they won't like it.

"My beloved has built many altars,
> and made them places for sinning instead
>> of cleansing.
I gave them my beautiful laws for their own good,
> yet they treated them like an affliction.
They still make sacrificial offerings,
> but with no regard for what I require.
> I do not accept them.
Their sacrifices are useless; they accomplish nothing!
> I will punish them.
> I will send them back to Egypt.
For they have utterly forgotten me.
> and focused on building palaces and fortresses
>> instead.
So I will send fire on their cities,
> and destruction on her fortifications."[15]

"I gave them my beautiful laws for their own good," God says in verse 12, "yet they treated them like an affliction." How often,

how habitually, is that true of me? I treat God's goodness to me like
an affliction.

How frustrated he must be when I approach his beautiful Word
as an obligation. How insulted he must feel when I refuse to come
to his banquet table. How horrible that I sometimes complain about
the job he has provided for me. How sad that I don't always give to
God with a cheerful heart.

I look everywhere else to fill my emptiness

The first verses of chapter 9 further underscore my resemblance to
the Israel of Hosea's day:

> Don't be so sure of yourself, Israel.
>> Don't act like you're as happy as everyone else,
>> sleeping around while forsaking your God.
> You've sold yourself everywhere you can,
>> but you're still hungry, aren't you?
> There's not enough wine in the world to fill
>> your emptiness.
> You won't be around much longer.
>> You'll be a slave to Egypt again;
>> you'll be Assyria's whore.
> Soon you won't be able to worship the Lord if you
>> wanted to;
>> even if you try, your offerings will be unclean,
> like moldy bread,
>> good for nothing and no one but yourself.
>
> What will your holidays and parties be like then?
> You may run, but you can't hide;
>> Egypt will find you,

and you'll be buried in the sands of Memphis.
Your silver will tarnish
    and your homes will crumble.
You won't be able to postpone punishment any longer;
    you'll have to pay for your sins.
You'll know: the prophets aren't as dumb as you think,
    the true worshipers of Yahweh won't look so foolish
when you are called to account for your great sin
    and hatefulness.[152]

We touched on this a little in the previous chapter, but it keeps coming around in Hosea's prophecy. Like Israel, I have an amazing capacity to look everywhere else but to God for fulfillment and satisfaction. I seek security in other things. I seek approval from other sources. I seek comfort in other ways. God may well say to me, as he tells Israel in Hosea 9:1b–2, "You've sold yourself everywhere you can, but you're still hungry, aren't you? There's not enough wine [money, possessions, food, etc.] in the world to fill your emptiness."

I may testify to the truth of the following words by the great preacher and scholar Jonathan Edwards, but I too seldom live them:

> God, *You are* the highest good of the reasonable creature, and the enjoyment of *You* is the only happiness with which our souls can be satisfied.
>
> To go to heaven fully to enjoy *You* is infinitely better than the most pleasant accommodations here.
>
> Fathers and mothers, husbands, wives, children, or the company of earthly friends, are but shadows. But the enjoyment of *You* is the substance.
>
> These are but scattered beams, but *You are* the sun.
>
> These are but streams, but *You are* the fountain.

These are but drops, but *You are* the ocean.

Amen.[153]

I reject correction

God's next words for Israel—and for me and you—highlight a rejection of counsel and correction:

> "The prophet is God's watchman over Israel;
> yet they are always trying to trap him,
>   pouring out hatred on him.
> They have deeply corrupted themselves
>   as in the days of Gibeah:
> he will remember their iniquity;
>   he will punish their sins."[154]

God sent prophets to his people, one after the other, and yet they were all treated harshly—such men and women as Deborah, Elijah, Elisha, and others. And, in Hosea's day, not only Hosea himself, but also Isaiah, Micah, and Amos were sent to prophesy to God's people. But the counsel and correction they offered were rejected . . . as is some of the godly counsel God sends my way these days.

I don't handle correction well. I know I am like the person addressed by Wisdom Incarnate in the first chapter of Proverbs:

> You should respond when I correct you.
>   Look, I'll pour out my spirit on you.
>   I'll reveal my words to you.
> I invited you, but you rejected me;
>   I stretched out my hand to you,
>   but you paid no attention.
> You ignored all my advice,

and you didn't want me to correct you.[155]

I don't want to be that guy, but I am, too often. I become defensive at the first sign of disagreement or correction. Something in me equates correction with rejection, at an almost primal level. You probably can't identify. But it makes it difficult for me to receive even the most loving, tactful efforts at counsel and correction.

Everyone in Hosea's audience would have instantly recognized the mention in verse 9 to the "days of Gibeah." It refers to incidents recorded in Judges 19, when the residents of that town brutalized a woman who was the concubine of a Levite who was traveling through the area. Rather than welcoming the Levite as a representative of God, they rejected him and his companion in the worst possible ways. The allusion would have conjured images of the most twisted, degenerate, villainous corruption.

You and I, of course, have done nothing so horrible as those men of Gibeah. But neither do we welcome prophets with difficult messages. We love our comfort. We cherish our self-esteem. We want positive messages. But that laziness of spirit will do us no good. We must learn to accept—invite, even—counsel and correction from God and his servants, or we will all the more likely sow the seeds of corruption in our souls.

I fail to be grateful

God's next words through his prophet Hosea go on to contrast his unfailing tenderness and kindness toward his people with their hideously ungrateful response:

> "Like one who finds grapes in the wilderness,
> I found Israel.
> Like one who sees the first fruit on a fig tree

I was delighted to see your fathers.
But they came to Baal-peor
    and bound themselves to a disgusting idol,
    and took on the stink of their vile partner.
Israel's glory will flutter off like a bird—
    they will have no births to celebrate,
and, worse,
    they will grieve the loss of their heirs.
They will be sorry
    that I have left them!
I knew my Israel
    when they were like a young palm planted in a
        pleasant place,
    but they are leading their children to destruction."

O Lord, I don't even know what to ask for such
        faithless people,
    except for wombs that won't give birth
    and breasts that won't give milk.

"From the beginning of our relationship,
    they treated me wickedly.
They worked overtime
    to earn my hatred and rejection.
I will give them what they want
    and let them follow their rebellious leaders.
My Israel is diseased;
    they are sick from the bottom of their hearts;
    there is no health in them.
Even if they manage to give birth,
    I will take their children away."

My God will turn his back on them
    who turned their hearts from him;
    they will be nomads.

Israel is a flourishing vine
    laden with fruit.
Yet the more they prosper,
    the more pagan altars they build.
The more prosperity,
    the more profligacy.
Their hearts are fickle;
    and no amount of pleading can ease their guilt."[156]

Notice the tenderness of God's attitude toward his people. He compares himself to a hungry traveler who finds grapes in the desert, and to someone who discovers tasty new fruit on a fig tree. He says, "They were like a young palm planted in a pleasant place."

But notice, too, the thanks God received from his beloved: they "bound themselves to a disgusting idol, and took on the stink of their vile partner." "They treated me wickedly. They worked overtime to earn my hatred and rejection." They built pagan altars. "Their hearts are fickle."

It is nothing short of amazing that the people of God would respond to his love and favor like that. But God has been no less tender, no less gracious, toward me. And I too seldom react with gratitude to his gifts. Morgan wrote, "The sin of a people of high privilege is the most heinous of which humanity is capable."[157] Is anyone more privileged than you and I?

I was exposed to the Gospel from an early age. I enjoyed the blessing of a Christian upbringing. I have known God's love from my earliest days. I have the Word of God, the blessed revelation of

God to man, available to me—in multiple translations and versions! I have never lacked Christian companionship. I am blessed with a lovely Christian wife and amazing children and grandchildren. I live in a prosperous country, "laden with fruit," so to speak. I enjoy innumerable creature comforts. I have freedoms and opportunities that others can only imagine. I have so much food to eat I keep gaining weight. And the list goes on. Yet, with so many blessings and privileges, I am irregular and fleeting in my gratitude to God.

A meme making its rounds of the Internet posed the question, "What if you woke up tomorrow with only the things you thanked God for today?" It drives home the point.

"Ah," you might say, "but if I truly gave thanks for all God's blessings, I would have no time for anything else. It would consume every waking moment." Exactly. That is how privileged we are—which makes any hesitation or inattention to expressing our gratitude more pronounced.

I break promises

Hosea 10:2b–4 continues the denunciation of Israel's behavior in the prophet's voice:

> Yahweh will smash their altars
> and demolish their idols.
>
> When that happens, they will say,
> "We have no god, we have no king,
> who is there to help us?"
> They will say anything
> to get what they want.
> They are quick to make promises,
> and quick to break them.

Disputes spring up among them
　　like noxious weeds in a plowed field.[158]

Hosea lists one flaw after another. "They will say anything to get what they want," he says, then goes on to point out their penchant for breaking promises and picking fights.

What would it look like if God kept track of the promises we made to him over the years? How would we fare if he suddenly "called in" all those vows and held us to our oaths? I don't know about you, but it's a frightening thought to me. I have, over the years, promised God much—and delivered little.

He is merciful and gracious, of course. He keeps no record of our wrongs. Those who are "in Christ Jesus" should have no fear of condemnation.[159] Nonetheless, it is a sobering thought—and one that ought to deliver us from any sense of self-righteousness—to reflect on the promises we have made and broken to our patient and loving God.

I cherish and defend idols

As Hosea's tenth chapter continues, the prophet pointedly addresses the people's idolatry. In addition to the golden calves King Jeroboam erected in Dan and Bethel as a substitute for worship at the temple of the Lord in Jerusalem, Hosea's contemporaries worshiped numerous other gods, particularly Baal, whose shrines seemed to decorate every hilltop:

They are so proud of their idols,
　　and get so worked up when anything threatens them.
But their idols will be boxed up and shipped off;
　　their pride will become their shame.
Those who led them in their idolatry will be swept away

like a twig floating downstream.
Their precious high places will be brought low.
    Weeds will grow up over their altars,
and they will try to hide themselves
    in their shame.

"From the very first, you have betrayed me, O Israel;
    and you have only continued in the way you began.
    And so it will be until the end.
So it will be until they receive what they deserve.
    Foreign armies will crush them
    for their repeated sin.[160]

We read such passages as those almost as if we are reading a foreign language. We don't identify with Israel's idolatry at all. We believe we are beyond that. Above that. But author and speaker Ed Stetzer writes,

> My idols are much more personal than a piece of stone
> or a block of wood. Anything from my past or present
> that shapes my identity or fills my thoughts with
> something other than God, especially on a regular,
> ongoing, irresistible basis, is an idol. Idolatry does not
> count the cost of worshipping anything but God. And
> although few of us could ever imagine worshipping
> a picture of ourselves, the reality is—we are either
> worshipping God or some form of ourselves. When
> we are driven by physical and emotional appetites
> rather than being led by the Spirit of God, we are
> worshipping the idol of ourselves. . . . Even many God-
> given desires can turn into idols when we become

Relearning What Love Is

too urgent to satisfy those desires. But every idol is a
competitor.[161]

Seen in that light, it should be hard *not* to identify with Israel's idol-
atry. In fact, it is my belief (as I wrote in my 2006 book, *American
Idols*) that we are at least as prone to idolatry as ancient Israel was.
The difference is that our idols are not personalities like Baal and
Molech; they are more often things like consumerism, comfort, suc-
cess, self-reliance, and, of course, money.

A funny thing happened in the writing of that book. Chapter
by chapter, I came under the conviction of the Holy Spirit. I realized that my heart is (to use Calvin's phrase) "a perpetual factory of
idols."[162] Worse, I have since come to realize that almost any time I
become defensive or angry, it is because one of my cherished idols
is being threatened in some ways. It happens more often than you
might think. It probably happens to you more than you think.

I trust myself

Hosea's tenth chapter closes with the following words:

> "My Israel was a tame calf that loved to serve her master,
>   and I treated her tenderly;
>   but no more.
> I will put a yoke on her neck,
>   and she will bend low under it.
> Oh, my people, sow righteousness,
>   reap love and mercy.
> Break up your fallow ground,
>   and seek Yahweh *now*,
>   that he may come and rain righteousness upon you.
> But you have scattered wickedness,

and so you have reaped ugliness;
     you have gorged yourself on lies.
You have trusted only in yourself
     and surrounded yourself with defenses.
But it will do you no good.
     Unimaginable destruction is coming your way,
     utter devastation.
It will be nothing you don't deserve,
     nothing your evil hasn't invited.
When that day dawns,
     all you have known will come to an end.[163]

In many ways, my journey of faith has been one long, winding path of learning to trust God rather than myself. I suppose that's true of everyone. But I suspect in this respect (among others) I am the chief of sinners.[164]

I am like a stubborn toddler who insists, "I can do it myself!" I am far too slow to turn to God. I tend to operate in my own strength until I make an absolute mess of things, and even then I am often slow to stop trusting in myself. Like Israel, I trust only in myself and surround myself with defenses. I have to; I need those defenses . . . for when my efforts come up short (and they always do).

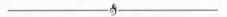

Hosea's prophecy helps me to see how my wayward soul must try the patience of God and grieve him to no end. How brokenhearted he must be when I allow myself to be misled by feelings and so miss his love for me, and the love I should have—and want to have—for him. How it must sadden him when I take his love for granted and scatter seeds of rebellion along my life's path. How it must wound him when I treat his goodness like affliction and look everywhere else for the satisfaction my soul craves—and which only he can give. How it must pain him when I reject his correction, fail to express my gratitude, break multiple promises, and cherish and defend my pitiful idols. And—especially after all that—how he must suffer to see me stubbornly, repeatedly trusting myself rather than turning to him.

When I consider how much like Israel I really am—and how unstintingly tender and patient he is with me, nonetheless—I cannot help but be "lost in wonder, love, and praise."[165] And move that much closer to falling utterly, passionately, irretrievably in love with God.

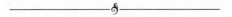

Lord God, Adonai, how tender and patient you are with me. And how insensitive I have been to the many ways in which I continue to fail to love you and serve you as you deserve. I want to be your constant, attentive, submissive, appreciative, grateful, receptive, and faithful child. How often have you warned me and sweetly invited me to respond to you? How slow have I been to recognize the hardness of my heart and obstinacy of my ways? How many times have I grieved you? Oh, Lord God, turn my heart to you. Draw me as you have never drawn me before. And give me the grace to respond more sweetly and completely than ever before, that I may find in you all my heart's desires. In Jesus' name, amen.

9

Climbing the
Heights of Love

"*Love Is a Many-Splendored Thing*," a song written in the 1950s by Sammy Fain and Paul Francis Webster, won the Academy Award for Best Original Song (from the movie of the same title) in 1955. It became a hit for The Four Aces, and has been recorded by such stars as Frank Sinatra, Andy Williams, Nat King Cole, Barry Manilow, and Ringo Starr. The song's lyrics compare love to "the April rose that only grows in the early spring" and to "the golden crown that makes a man a king." "Yes," its final line says, "true love's a many-splendored thing."

As schmaltzy as the song may sound, lyricist Paul Francis Webster had it right. So did Elizabeth Barrett Browning in her Sonnet 43, the next to last of her forty-four *Sonnets from the Portuguese:*

> How do I love thee? Let me count the ways.
> I love thee to the depth and breadth and height
> My soul can reach, when feeling out of sight

For the ends of Being and ideal Grace.
I love thee to the level of everyday's
Most quiet need, by sun and candle-light.
I love thee freely, as men strive for Right;
I love thee purely, as they turn from Praise.
I love thee with a passion put to use
In my old griefs, and with my childhood's faith.
I love thee with a love I seemed to lose
With my lost saints,—I love thee with the breath,
Smiles, tears, of all my life!—and, if God choose,
I shall but love thee better after death.[166]

Browning's poem (written for her then-fiancé Robert Browning) depicts some of the many facets of true love: deep, broad, high; freely, purely, passionately; with breath, smiles, tears, and more.

As I mentioned earlier, my wife and I were married when we were both nineteen years old—three years after we began dating. At the time of our wedding, I thought I knew what love was. I was sure I loved her to the depth and breadth and height my soul could reach, as Browning said. She was to me a best friend, boon companion, confidante, lover, teacher, conscience, muse. However, several decades later, I know that on my wedding day I had only begun to understand and appreciate the "depth and breadth and height" of love.

If that is true of human love, how much more must it be true of God's love? If romantic love is "a many-splendored thing," what phrase could possibly be used to describe the splendors of God's love?

More Than You Know

After ten chapters in which God, through his prophet Hosea, described his love for Israel primarily in terms of the love between a long-suffering husband and an unfaithful wife, he takes a notable and significant turn in the eleventh chapter. As deep and wide and high as the love between a husband and wife is, it takes more to express God's love for his people. A single metaphor can communicate much, but in Hosea's eleventh chapter, we are confronted with a series of metaphors to help us appreciate the many-splendored nature of God's love for us. In one of the most tender chapters of the Old Testament—of the entire Bible, in fact—God expresses his feelings for Israel . . . and, in so doing, illuminates his feelings for you and me.

I am loved like a son

Chapter 11 opens with God referring to Israel as a son:

> "When Israel was a child, I loved him.
>> I called them out of Egypt like a midwife coaxing an
>>> infant from the womb.
> But the more lovingly I spoke to them,
>> the farther they ran away;
> they played with their Baals on the hills
>> and burned offerings to idols.
> It was I who had taught them to walk;
>> I cradled them in my arms,
>>> but they did not know that I was the one who kissed
>>>> their boo-boos."[167]

The first verses of Hosea 11 mark the third time the prophet has returned to the early days of Israel (Hosea 9:10, 10:1). In these verses, of course, he refers to the Exodus, the momentous series of events when God sent Moses to lead the enslaved Hebrews out of Egypt. It is an echo of the message God told Moses to deliver to Pharaoh: "Israel is My son, even My firstborn . . . let My son go, that he may worship me."[168]

God not only guided them out of hardship and affliction, "like a midwife coaxing an infant from the womb," he cradled and nurtured them when they were too weak to stand on their own. He taught them their first steps. He "kissed their boo-boos." He parallels their exodus from Egypt and early days as a nation with a father's love for a not-yet-born and just-born child through the toddler's first brave steps.

God loves you and me like that. Whether you are male or female, he loves you like a son. Like a firstborn son. Like an only son. The psalmist's realization ought to be yours as well:

> You created my inmost being;
>> you knit me together in my mother's womb. . . .
> My frame was not hidden from you
>> when I was made in the secret place,
>> when I was woven together in the depths of the earth.
> Your eyes saw my unformed body;
>> all the days ordained for me were written in your book
>> before one of them came to be.[169]

God loved you when your form was being molded. He loved you before you were known to anyone else. He loved you before you knew anything about love. And his love for you has only grown since then. Anne Lamott, in her book *Operating Instructions*, wrote,

> One thing about having a baby, is that each step of the way you simply cannot imagine loving him any more than you already do, because you are bursting with love, loving as much as you are humanly capable of— and then you do, you love him even more.[170]

Can you imagine? God loves you like that. He is bursting with love, loving as much as he is capable of—and he is infinitely more capable of love than any human parent.

So it is. I am loved like a son. You are loved like a son. And even that merely scratches the surface.

I am loved like a pet

It may seem like something of a comedown to say, "God loves me like a pet," especially after considering the fact that God loves us like a father loves a son. But it's not. The purpose is not to improve upon the previous image, but to present another perspective, another facet of his love for his beloved. In ancient Israel, as in our day, there were people who would have struggled to identify with the love of a father for a son (to quote Anne Lamott again, "I don't remember who said this, but there really are places in the heart you don't even know exist until you love a child").[171] Even a child or a childless adult, however, could identify with the depiction of his love in Hosea 11:4–7:

> "I led them tenderly, with cords of kindness,
>   as one guides a pet around a yard.
> I loosened the harness so it wouldn't rub,
>   and fed them by hand.
>
> "They will not return to slavery in Egypt

> but they will end up in bondage to Assyria
>> rather than return to me.
> Violence rages in their cities,
>> enemies devour them left and right
>> because of their foolish plans,
> yet they are hell-bent on rejecting me.
>> Now, if they were to call out to me,
>> it would be no use."[172]

God says of his people, "I led them tenderly, with cords of kindness, as one guides a pet around a yard." The most familiar pet to Hosea's first audience probably would have been a lamb or a calf. It is much the same image as the one used in the previous chapter: "My Israel was a tame calf that loved to serve her master."[173] Anyone who has ever loved—or lost—a family pet can attest to the depth of love that exists in such a relationship.

The tender imagery continues as God is described as loosening the harness on the pet's head and feeding it by hand. It is a picture of gentleness and sensitivity, like that in Dorothy Thrupp's hymn:

> Savior, like a shepherd lead us, much we need Thy
>> tender care;
> In Thy pleasant pastures feed us, for our use Thy
>> folds prepare.
> Blessèd Jesus, blessèd Jesus! Thou hast bought us, Thine
>> we are.
>
> We are Thine, do Thou befriend us, be the guardian of
>> our way;
> Keep Thy flock, from sin defend us, seek us when we
>> go astray.

Blessèd Jesus, blessèd Jesus! Hear, O hear us when
we pray.

Thou hast promised to receive us, poor and sinful though
we be;
Thou hast mercy to relieve us, grace to cleanse and power
to free.
Blessèd Jesus, blessèd Jesus! We will early turn to Thee.

Early let us seek Thy favor, early let us do Thy will;
Blessèd Lord and only Savior, with Thy love our
bosoms fill.
Blessèd Jesus, blessèd Jesus! Thou hast loved us, love us still.[174]

But again, after using the most tender imagery, God must remind his people that, as kind and gentle as his ministrations have been, they have all been rejected in the worst possible ways. When he says, "They will not return to slavery in Egypt but they will end up in bondage to Assyria" in verse 5, he evokes their past deliverance while foretelling their future oppression. In those words, we may also find a challenge, for how often do we, even today, experience deliverance from one form of bondage only to slide into another? How often have I—who have experienced God's free and full salvation—ended up in bondage to some new affliction?

Still, God loves me, like a silly lamb or a stumbling calf, caring for me as sweetly as any prized pet.

I am loved like a rock

It ought to move us and bless us to know that God loves us like a son and cares for us like a coddled house pet. But there is still another aspect of God's love, described in verses 8–9:

"How can I give you up, my Israel?
  How can I let you go?
How can I watch you be ruined?
  How can I endure your destruction?
My heart breaks;
  my compassion rekindles.
How can I carry out my anger?
  I will not destroy my Israel;
for I am God and not a man,
  I am the Holy One in your midst,
  and I will not utterly destroy you."[175]

American singer and songwriter Paul Simon (half of the Simon & Garfunkel duo) scored a hit song in 1973 with "Loves Me Like a Rock," which was given a gospel flavor by the accompanying vocals of the Dixie Hummingbirds. The song's title refers to a mother's rock-solid love for her son.

That is very much the imagery of Hosea 11:8–9. Like a long-suffering mother, God asks a series of impossible questions, one after the other. How can I give you up? How can I let you go? How can I watch you be ruined? How can I endure your destruction? How can I carry out my anger? The unspoken answer to each, of course, is, "I can't. I love you too much." Though his heart is breaking, his compassion prevents him from destroying his beloved.

The reason he gives for not destroying Israel as he had long before destroyed Sodom and Gomorrah and other cities of the plains[176] is, "I am God and not a man; I am the Holy One in your midst." One ancient rabbi translated the latter phrase as, "God is Israel's heart." In other words, "I am in you. I am a part of you. My life is intertwined with your life."

So it is with you and me. God's love for you is rock solid. The words of an old prayer chorus are true of me. And of you:

> He cannot forget me, though trials beset me,
> For ever His promise shall stand.
> He cannot forget me, though trials beset me,
> My name's on the palm of his hand.[177]

I am loved like a lion

Throughout the metaphors of Hosea 11, God loosely tracked Israel's history as he communicated his love for them. In Israel's nascency in Egypt, God loved them as a father loves a son. Throughout their history, he cared for them like a child tending to a favorite pet. Even in their apostasy, he loved them like a rock. And then, in the final scene of chapter 11, he employs one more image:

> You will follow me again.
> I will roar like a lion,
> > and my children will come trembling from a distance;
> they will fly back to me like birds from Egypt,
> > and like doves from Assyria,
> and I will restore them to their homes, I promise.[178]

The first image in these verses is of a mother lion, whose cubs have strayed too far from the den. So she summons them with a mighty roar and brings them back to the safety of the pride. So, God says, will he summon his beloved ones and gather them to himself once more.

It is a reference, of course, to the approaching apocalypse of the Assyrian and Babylonian captivities, when the people of God would be carried off into exile for many years. But at the end of that time—as recorded in the books of Ezra and Nehemiah in our Bibles—God would bring his people together again.

God loves you like that. However often and far you may stray from him, he will beckon you back. He loves you like a lion. He calls you over and over again, sometimes with lullaby tones and at other times with a fierce roar.

The great nineteenth-century preacher Dwight L. Moody told the story of a father who worked a farm on the American prairies. In those days, before the railroad reached to the prairies, the grain had to be shipped in wagons for hundreds of miles to Chicago, where it was then loaded onto ships that plied the Great Lakes.

This father, who was a preacher as well as a farmer, came to be detained by church business, so he sent his son to Chicago with the grain in a wagon, pulled by a team of strong horses. He waited for the boy to return, but he never did. Finally, desperate, the father saddled his horse and rode to the place he had sent his son. He asked around, and learned that his son had been there and had sold the grain. Fearing that his boy had been robbed and perhaps murdered for the money, he hired a detective who tracked the boy to a gambling den. There, he learned that the boy had gambled away all the money and, in an attempt to win it back, sold the horses and wagon. He lost that money, too, and then disappeared.

The father went looking for his son. He went from town to town. When he entered a new town, he would prevail upon the local ministers to let him preach, and, at the close of his sermon, he would tell his story, concluding, "If you ever see him or hear of him, will you write to me?"

At some point he heard that the boy had gone to California, thousands of miles away. So the father traveled to San Francisco and made arrangements to preach there. He advertised in newspapers in the hope that his son would see the advertisement and come to hear him.

When he finished preaching, he once again told his son's story and issued the same appeal. When the service ended and the audience filed out, he noticed one young man who held back until the crowd was gone. It was his son. The father ran to him, like the prodigal's father he was, and pressed his son to his bosom.

God loves you. Like a son. A firstborn son. An only son.

God loves you. Like a favorite pet. A coddled lamb or a clumsy calf.

God loves you. Like a rock. Immovable. Immense. Unchanging.

God loves you. Like a lion. Roaring. Waiting. Intent on your return.

---

§

God, your love is amazing. Thank you for showing to me, through your prophet Hosea, the many facets of your love for me. You knew me and loved me before I was even born. You loved me from the moment of my first breath. You loved me in my sin. You loved me and gave your Son for me. You loved me in Christ. You loved me in all my waywardness. You loved me in all my clumsy attempts to please you. You loved me like a rock. You loved me steadfastly. You loved me like a lion, calling me back to your side. You love me still. You will love me ever. Thank you for your unfathomable love, from before the foundation of the world until now. Teach me to love you more truly. In Jesus' name, amen.

10

Returning
to Love

*M*y wife, *the lovely Robin,* and I left immediately after church that Sunday with our twenty-year-old son, Aaron. We were headed for Florida from our home in southwestern Ohio.

Our 1997 Dodge Caravan, with 128,000 miles on the odometer, was packed about as full as an Elvis impersonator in a white sequined suit. We drove to Atlanta that day, then to the Orlando area the next, and spent almost a week settling our son into a new apartment, a new school, and a new phase in his life. We scrubbed floors and appliances, bought used furniture, stocked the cupboards with groceries, and hung posters on the walls.

Then, that next Saturday, the lovely Robin and I left our hotel at 7 A.M. and started the long drive home: fifteen hours, with just a few stops for the necessary things of life—M&Ms and Diet Mountain Dew, mostly. But the trip went well, except that it seemed so much longer than the trip down—return trips usually do—and for the last hour or two, late Saturday night, it seemed we would never get back . . . a sensation, an experience, that has its parallel in the spiritual life.

Return to Love

Even the most tender heart towards God sometimes drifts—not intentionally, of course. More often, it is simply the result of being human. There are so many things vying for our attention and affection. The unpredictability of daily life may upset our rhythms and disrupt our communications with God. Each day presents a thousand tiny opportunities to inch away from the God who loves us so freely, purely, and passionately, like a devoted husband, doting father, and tender shepherd.

The ancient prophecy of this guy named Hosea who, in obedience to God, not only married a promiscuous woman, but let himself be hurt again and again by her unfaithfulness as a vivid illustration of God's love for us, has more left to teach us. It can map for us the return trip of a heart like mine, a heart that so often strays from God's embrace—not every once in a while, but daily, many times daily. It can help us return and keep returning to the God who keeps drawing us back with "ropes of kindness and love."[179] Beginning with the last verse of Hosea's eleventh chapter and continuing into chapter 12, we will explore how to return—no matter how far, no matter how long ago or how recently, no matter how little or much we may have fallen out of love with God. And though it may seem the return trip is a long way, the route is clearly marked for us all, in something like a biblical GPS device.

It is a trip any one of us can take. And it is never too late. Nor is it ever too early. And it can be traversed over and over again.

I will recognize what is

The last verse of Hosea 11 through the first two verses of the twelfth chapter says this:

> My Israel has encircled me
>> with lies and pretense.
> And Judah is out of control,
>> repeatedly running away from my faithful love.
>
> My Israel tries to gorge themselves on emptiness,
>> and sucks wind all day;
> they add falsehood to falsehood
>> and multiply it with violence;
> they treaty with Assyria,
>> and trade with Egypt.
>
> Yahweh has filed charges against them.
>> They will be punished;
>> they will pay.[180]

To return the gracious, stubborn, unconditional love of God, even when we've gone far astray, we must first recognize what is. We must face where we are. God wants honest hearts, honest responses from us. That is what it takes to return God's love. It takes a heart that is willing to take a good hard look at its own condition.

God said, through his prophet Hosea, that his people, Israel, had surrounded him with lies and pretense. And Judah, the southern kingdom, was "out of control," or, as the New International Version has it, "unruly." The word in Hebrew was commonly used to refer to cattle that habitually broke loose from the safety and comfort of their pens—much like my heart, which identifies with the words of Robert Robinson in the hymn "Come Thou Fount of Every Blessing":

> Prone to wander, Lord, I feel it,
> Prone to leave the God I love.[181]

God goes on to say, "My Israel tries to gorge themselves on emptiness." A friend of mine was frustrated a few years ago by a horse of his that started a practice called "cribbing," or "windsucking." The horse would anchor its top front teeth on a fencepost or rail, arch its neck, and draw in great gulps of air, filling its belly, until he felt full and bloated—though, of course, he had taken in no nourishment at all. My friend tried everything he could to make the creature stop, but it was all to no avail. In fact, many experts say it is impossible to cure; it is believed that the practice releases endorphins into the horse's system, making it pleasurable, and actually creating an addiction. Tragically, a horse will sometimes do this so often and for so long that it ends up dying of malnutrition.

That's what it is like for the heart that is wandering from God, that has run from him and blocked out his loving entreaties. It is sucking air, gorging on emptiness, trying to satisfy the hunger inside only to become more and more starved, more and more emaciated in spirit. Maybe you don't know what that's like, but I do. I know what it's like to "gorge on emptiness" and "suck wind," even though I know—I truly know—that in God, "My soul will be satisfied as with the richest of foods."[182] I have "tasted that the Lord is good."[183] I have "tasted the heavenly gift."[184] I have "tasted the goodness of the word of God."[185]

And yet, every so often, I stop and take an honest look at where my life is, what I'm doing day after day, where I'm putting my effort and attention; and if I'm honest with myself, if I recognize what

really is, I see that like an unruly calf—or a windsucking horse—
I've bolted from the lush pasture of my Master and have been filling
my belly with emptiness. So it's no wonder, no wonder at all, that
my life has been producing bad fruit, lies and violence, and double-
mindedness, like King Hoshea of Israel who tried to make a treaty
with Assyria while dealing under the table with Egypt.[186]

When I stop to recognize what is, I can see so clearly that the
Lord has a charge to bring against me and would be thoroughly
reasonable in punishing me accordingly, as Hosea 12:2 says. And
some of us stop there. We recognize where we are, but we figure,
"No, it's too hard," or, "It'll cost too much," or, "It'll take too long"
to return God's patient, stubborn, unconditional love. That's why
God, through Hosea, gave us the next three verses in chapter 12.

Review what has been

In Hosea 12:3–5, the prophet draws a parallel between God's
people, his beloved, and their ancestor Jacob, whose story is recorded
in the book of Genesis:

> Their ancestor fought with his brother in the womb,
>> and wrestled with God in the night.
> He struggled, and won;
>> he wept and found blessing.
> He met God there,
>> and God met him,
> Yahweh, the Almighty God,
>> whose name is forever.[187]

God is saying to his people, "Look, here's where you are! You're
deceitful! You're chronically unfaithful! You're trying to fill yourself
but only becoming more and more empty! But remember Jacob?

There was no one more deceitful than him—even in the *womb* he was a deceiver! Yet, as a man, he wrestled with God—and *won*! He prevailed! He received his heart's desire from God! He was not disappointed. Remember?"

As you read those verses about Jacob (whose name became Israel after he wrestled with God), God may be saying to you, "Look, you can learn from the example of others. Look at Jacob. God had every reason to reject him . . . but he didn't." He may be saying, "Look at Ruth. Look at David. Look at Peter. Look around you at the God-lovers you know. Do you know their stories? Do you know what God has brought them from? Do you know where God is taking them? Consider what God has done for them as an indication of what he might do for you."

Or he might be saying, "Remember the height from which you have fallen!"[188] Remember when you prayed to God, and he answered. Remember when you wept and begged his favor, and he blessed you. Remember when you found him at your own Peniel and talked with him there and felt close to him and hungered for his presence and swore that if you had to, you would sell everything you had just to gain the pearl of great price, the awesome treasure he was to you.

If you find yourself thinking the journey back isn't worth it, or that it's too far or too hard, or that it's too *anything*, just review what has been, and you will do whatever you must do.

Reclaim what can be

God says to his people through Hosea, "Look at where you are," in Hosea 11:12–12:2. Then he says, "But remember what has been," in verses 3–5. And then, in verse 6, one of those beautiful, buried treasures that are found throughout Scripture, he says:

Do likewise!
>> Call on God! Struggle with him!
>> Wrestle with love and justice,
>> and don't give up.[189]

The New Living Translation renders those lines:

>> So now, come back to your God.
>> Act with love and justice,
>> and always depend on him.[190]

The New Century Version puts it this way:

>> You must return to your God;
>> love him, do what is just,
>> and always trust in him as your God.[191]

Whatever the version, the prophet says three things to the people of God that are likewise important for us today to hear and to heed.

Call on God, he says. No matter how far it may seem, you don't have to go far. It is like a science fiction portal that will transport you instantaneously to where you want to be, though you may have traveled an immense distance for a long time to get where you are. You don't have to go far because God has been pacing you, pursuing you, all along—as Simon Tugwell says:

> So long as we imagine that it is we who have to look
> for God, we must often lose heart. But it is the other
> way about; He is looking for us. And so we can afford
> to recognize that very often we are not looking for
> God; far from it, we are in full flight from him, in high
> rebellion against him. And he knows that and has

taken it into account. He has followed us into our own darkness; there where we thought finally to escape him, we run straight into his arms. So we do not have to erect a false piety for ourselves, to give us the hope of salvation. Our hope is in his determination to save us, and he will not give in.[192]

"Do like Jacob," Hosea cries. "Just do it!" he might have said. As Jesus said in The Revelation to his wayward followers at Ephesus, "Turn back! . . . No time to waste."[193] Or, in Isaiah's words, "Turn to the LORD, and he will have mercy on [you], and to our God, for he will freely pardon."[194]

Simply come to him in honesty, humility, repentance (that is, a willingness to turn from your sin and waywardness), and acceptance of his freely offered forgiveness and restoration, and he will receive you.

Wrestle with love and justice. Hosea has been talking about the story of Jacob, remember? Jacob was born clutching his twin brother Esau's heel and as an adult swindled his brother out of his birthright and blessing and had to flee for his life—or his brother may well have killed him. Maybe you've had a brother like that. Maybe you've *been* a brother like that.

In any case, years later, Jacob was again fleeing for his life, but this time was running from his father-in-law, back in the direction of his brother, Esau. On the night before Jacob was to be reunited with his brother—who for all he knew was still willing to kill him—Jacob had a life-changing encounter with God:

> That night Jacob got up and took his two wives, his two female servants and his eleven sons and crossed the ford of the Jabbok. After he had sent them

across the stream, he sent over all his possessions. So
Jacob was left alone, and a man wrestled with him
till daybreak. When the man saw that he could not
overpower him, he touched the socket of Jacob's
hip so that his hip was wrenched as he wrestled
with the man. Then the man said, "Let me go, for it
is daybreak."

But Jacob replied, "I will not let you go unless
you bless me."

The man asked him, "What is your name?"

"Jacob," he answered.

Then the man said, "Your name will no longer be
Jacob, but Israel, because you have struggled with God
and with humans and have overcome."

Jacob said, "Please tell me your name."

But he replied, "Why do you ask my name?" Then he
blessed him there.

So Jacob called the place Peniel, saying, "It is because
I saw God face to face, and yet my life was spared."

The sun rose above him as he passed Peniel, and he
was limping because of his hip.[195]

When morning came, Jacob came away from that place with
a new life and a new name: Israel. The old deceiver was gone, and,
when he finally met his brother, there was a new honesty in him, a
humility, a gentleness and tenderness he had never shown before.
Why? How? Because, in wrestling with God he had wrestled with
love and justice itself.

And so it will be with you. When you truly and sincerely return
to God, you may expect him to exact his "pound of flesh," so to

speak. You may fear that he will make you pay for having strayed from him and hurt him as you did. But, when you wrestle with God, you wrestle with love. He will not crush you.

But wrestling with the God of love and justice will *change* you. The Bible says that God, in his wrestling match with Jacob, "struck Jacob on the hip and threw it out of joint."[196] That may seem like poor sportsmanship, but it's not. The apparent purpose was to bring about a change. Moments later, Jacob was no longer "Jacob," which meant "liar" or "pretender" (like the Lord's complaints about his people in Hosea 11:12); God changed his name to Israel, which meant "God-wrestler."

When you truly return to God it will, of course, change you. It should breed not only love and justice but also humility and compassion—in fact, all the fruits of the Spirit.

Don't give up. Let's take one more look at Hosea 12:6. After setting up Jacob as an example, it says,

> Do likewise!
> > Call on God! Struggle with him!
> > Wrestle with love and justice,
> > and don't give up.[197]

The New Living Translation renders that last phrase,

> Always live in confident dependence on your God.[198]

That expresses it. That's the key to the whole thing.

You see, we read the verse, "Taste and see that the LORD is good,"[199] and we think, yeah, like a little kid that doesn't know how good Campbell's Soup is; once he tastes it, he knows: "That's what Campbell's Soup is, mm, mm good." (If you're not old enough to recognize that commercial jingle, that's your own fault.)

But I don't relate that verse to just tasting once and concluding the Lord is good. No, because I get hungry a mere two hours after every meal. (Ask my wife if I'm lying!) I relate that verse, "Taste and see that the LORD is good," to my constant, almost unremitting need for nourishment. I don't expect to eat once a week, or even once a day, and say, "Mm, that was good." I need my six square meals a day.

And I've discovered it's no different in my life with God. I need regular nourishment. I need to never give up. I need to always live in confident dependence on my God.

That's what rekindling the romance involves: a daily, even several times daily returning, returning, returning, because I'm hungry and he alone can satisfy my soul "as with the richest of foods."[200]

Wherever you are in your spiritual journey right now, I urge you to try this. Whatever your prayer habit has been, however far you may think you've gotten off track in your relationship with God, why not start today to reclaim what can be:

- return to God, in honesty and humility;
- surrender whatever bitterness or resentment you may be holding onto, and ask God to produce a new love and justice in your heart, a new love for him, a new enthusiasm for him; and then
- start living in confident dependence on your God. . . . If you've never been in the habit of praying, start praying every day; it doesn't have to be fancy, it can just be "God, help me."

If you've lost the habit of prayer, go back to what you were doing. If you've been praying something like daily, give God more than you have been giving him lately, and seek to increase your dependence on him.

I have a friend who realized as a teenager that if he didn't hurry through a perfunctory prayer as he said grace over a meal but, instead, chose to simply take the time to slow down, focus his thoughts on God, and spend even just three minutes in communion with him before he ate, he'd never go more than a few waking hours without prayerful dependence on God. It really can be that simple.

You really *can* stop sucking air, hungrily trying to fill the emptiness inside only to become more and more starved, more and more emaciated in spirit. . . .

You really can return.

You really can.

You can.

———————————— ♪ ————————————

Lord, God of love and justice, I am prone to wander, prone to leave the God I love. I come to you all too aware of my own waywardness, but more aware (I hope) of your mercy and grace. I would prevail upon you. I will keep wrestling with you. I will not give up. I will not let you go until you bless me.[201] *Turn my heart, Lord, like a stream of water; guide it wherever you like.*[202] *Help me to live in confident, constant dependence on you. In Jesus' name, amen.*

11

Letting Love
Change You

*L*ina Ng was awarded first runner-up in a 1993 version of *Star Search*, a network television show that was a forerunner to more recent shows like *American Idol* and *The Voice*.

You might think the Singapore native would have felt pretty good about not only being on TV but also going so far and achieving so much in the competition.

But she didn't.

There were rumors that she didn't win the title because "she wasn't pretty enough." Lina felt disappointed and bitter. She thought about having breast implants. She considered having her teeth fixed.

In the end, she did neither. She determined that she would just have to stay "not pretty enough."

But then—

She met Mike Lam. She fell in love. *He* fell in love. "Mike really changed my life," she says. "He made me believe in myself."

Lina became a completely changed woman. She exuded self-confidence. She felt pretty. She *was* pretty, though she never had the implants or the dental work. She didn't need them. Love transformed her. Love healed her and gave her a new confidence.

Back to Love

We've covered a lot of ground in this book, from exploring how God's heart hurts when we betray his gracious love to discovering how short a trip it is to return to God's love. In this chapter, I hope to show that what happened to Lina Ng—who, by the way, is also a follower of Jesus Christ—can happen in me and in you as a result of letting ourselves be changed by God's love.

The nearly three-thousand-year-old prophecy of Hosea is not too different from a roller coaster ride; it goes up and down, around and around, and eventually comes back to where it began. Many times throughout the book, God says to his people, "I've had it with you!" And then he says, "Please come back to my love." And then he says, "I will take you back and we'll be happy once again."

And Hosea 13 and 14 are no different. The first part of chapter 13 says,

> There once was a time when the word of my people
> > meant something;
> > they were respected,
> > but all that was lost through sin.
> And now there is no end to their sin.
> > They manufacture idols,
> > and craft them carefully,
> > as if it matters what kind of cow an idolater kisses.
> They are now like the morning mist
> > like the dew the sun chases away,

like chaff that is blown by the wind

    or smoke that fades into the atmosphere.

"But I am Yahweh,

    the God who rescued you from Egypt;

I am the only true God,

    for there is no other savior besides me.

I was the one who knew you in the desert,

    in those waterless tracts;

yet when you filled your bellies,

    you puffed out your chest and forgot all about me.

So I will be a lion to you;

    I will stalk you like a leopard.

I will pounce on you like an angry she-bear;

    I will rip and tear,

    and devour and destroy.

"Who will help you then, my Israel?

    Who will rescue you when I, who have been

        your helper,

    turn against you?

Will your king save you?

    What about your nobles?

You asked for a king to rule you,

    and I gave you what you wanted,

    until I took him away in my anger.

Your accounts are coming due;

    payment will be required.

You will be like a baby, reluctant to be born,

    who must be ripped from the womb.[203]

Much of it he has said before, in one way or another. As God had the poor prophet Hosea illustrate with his life, marriage, and experience, time and time again, God's beloved bride had taken him for granted and betrayed him and broken his heart.

Just like me.

Just like you, if you're anything like me . . . if you're anything like the rest of the human race.

But in spite of all that, God makes three amazing promises to his people that, much like a rousing symphony, form a fitting finale to this ancient story of love, betrayal, forgiveness, and restoration. They are promises that apply not only to the ancient nation of Israel—because Hosea is not just some storyteller, but a prophet—but to you and me today. And they are promises that have the potential to utterly transform our lives if we let them.

Let God's love deliver you

After detailing how Israel has sinned against him, how they have betrayed him, taken him for granted, and broken his heart, God says in Hosea 13:14:

> However, I will yet ransom you from the grave.
>> I will redeem you from Death.
>> I will say, "Where is your power now, Death?
>> Where is your sting, Grave?"
>
> And nothing will change my mind.[204]

In spite of all their sin, though they had spit in the eye of God, though they had betrayed him as horribly as a wife who jumps into another man's bed, God said,

> I will yet ransom you from the grave.
> I will redeem you from Death.[205]

And he did. He fulfilled that promise, not only to them but to you and me, when "the Son of Man [came] . . . to give his life as a ransom for many."[206]

As Paul the great church planter wrote to his young trainee, Titus:

> Once we, too, were foolish and disobedient. We were misled by others and became slaves to many wicked desires and evil pleasures. Our lives were full of evil and envy. We hated others, and they hated us.
>
> But then God our Savior showed us his kindness and love. He saved us, not because of the good things we did, but because of his mercy. He washed away our sins and gave us a new life through the Holy Spirit. He generously poured out the Spirit upon us because of what Jesus Christ our Savior did. He declared us not guilty because of his great kindness. And now we know that we will inherit eternal life.[207]

Did you catch all that? God's love delivers you from,

- wicked desires and evil pleasures
- Envy and hate
- The guilt of all your sins
- All the punishment those sins deserve
- The power of the grave
- Death itself!

God's love ransoms. Redeems. Delivers. As Mike Lam's love did for Lina Ng, it saves us from trying to "fix" what's wrong with us and breathes new life into every corner of our lives. It makes us beautiful. It makes us confident. It makes us optimistic.

But maybe you don't *feel* "delivered." Maybe you don't *feel* ransomed or redeemed. Maybe it doesn't seem real in your life. There can be several reasons for this.

1. You've never truly surrendered your life to God in Christ. The love of God is no more than an abstraction to the person who hasn't experienced new life in Jesus Christ. All the relief and freedom Paul lists in the passage above applies only to those who have received "new life through the Holy Spirit." There is no other way to experience that deliverance. If that describes the desire of your heart, if that's a need you feel right now, then you can begin by praying a simple prayer of faith, like this:

> *Jesus, I admit that I've disobeyed you;*
> *I've been a slave to wicked desires;*
> *I've done all sorts of wrong things.*
> *But you've promised to save me.*
> *You've promised to ransom and redeem me,*
> *and so I ask for your forgiveness.*
> *I believe that you died for me,*
> *and I want to turn from my sins.*
> *I now invite you to come into my heart*
> *and take control of my life from now on.*
> *In Jesus' name, amen.*

Now, if you've sincerely prayed that prayer, the Bible says that everything Paul said in Titus 3:3–7 is true ... of you! You are delivered from all wicked desires and evil pleasures, envy and hate, the guilt of all your sins, the punishment those sins deserve, the power of the grave, and from death itself! Which is what prompted Paul, in 1 Corinthians 15, to paraphrase Hosea's prophecy, saying,

"Where, O death, is your victory?
Where, O death, is your sting?"
The sting of death is sin, and the power of sin is
the law. But thanks be to God! He gives us the victory
through our Lord Jesus Christ.[208]

But there may be other reasons you don't "feel" delivered.

2. You're relying on feelings. The truth of the matter is you will never feel delivered by focusing your attention on feeling delivered. C. S. Lewis emphasized this in his justifiably famous book *The Screwtape Letters.* The book is presented as a series of letters from Screwtape, an experienced demon, to his less experienced nephew, Wormwood. Writing of the human beings who are the subjects of their temptations, Screwtape writes,

> Whenever they are attending to the Enemy Himself
> we are defeated, but there are ways of preventing them
> from doing so. The simplest is to turn their gaze away
> from Him towards themselves. Keep them watching
> their own minds and trying to produce *feelings* there
> by the action of their own wills. . . . Teach them to
> estimate . . . their success in producing the desired
> feeling; and never let them suspect how much success
> or failure of that kind depends on whether they are
> well or ill, fresh or tired, at the moment.[209]

Several years ago, I was—for the first time in my life—depressed. Under the guidance of a counselor, I did numerous things to overcome the depression,[210] but I'm convinced the most effective things I did were affirmation and thanksgiving. That is, I devoted chunks of time to prayer, and in many of those prayer times I repeated such truths as "My help is in the name of the Lord, the Maker of heaven and earth."[211] I also focused my prayers on giving detailed thanks for the many blessings I enjoy in my life. I began recording in my journal at least three things every night for which I was thankful. Since Mondays were often my lowest days, I committed to focusing on giving thanks every Monday, turning it into a weekly "mini-Thanksgiving Day." These measures (and others) turned my gaze off of me and my circumstances and focused it on God and his love and truth.

Likewise, you will "feel" delivered as you focus intently on God and his truth, rather than on what you feel.

3. You're bowing to idols. No one will truly grasp the deliverance that is ours in Christ Jesus who is trying to please someone or something other than God. It is no coincidence that so much of God's word through Hosea shines a light on the depth of Israel's idolatry. You just can't experience deliverance and freedom while you are bowing to an idol—whether that idol is sex, money, success, convenience, or your mother-in-law's approval. If Hosea teaches us anything, it must be this: idols must go before we can fall in love with God and experience the joy and freedom of that kind of relationship with him. (And we all struggle with idols, some more subtle than others; for that reason, I recommend my book *American Idols*, which identifies fourteen of our most common idols, as well as steps to take to cast down those idols.)

4. You're enslaved by old beliefs or habits. The great reformer Martin Luther, commenting on the line in the Lord's Prayer that asks, "Lead us not into temptation," wrote, "We pray in this petition that God would guard and keep us lest the devil, the world, and our flesh lead us into misbelief, despair and other great shame and vice."[212] Old, ingrained beliefs and habits should be examined and, when they don't correspond to the truth of the Gospel of Jesus Christ, they need to be systematically countered. So, for example, if you are in the habit of telling yourself (consciously or unconsciously), "I'm no good, I can't do this," you might meditate daily on Ephesians 2:10 ("For we are God's masterpiece")[213] or Philippians 4:13 ("I can do all things through Christ who strengthens me").[214] You might also read William Backus and Marie Chapian's book, *Telling Yourself the Truth*, which gives further instruction on deliverance from old beliefs or habits. In some cases, of course, you should seek help from others, such as a wise counselor or a support group.

Whatever the obstacles, the truth is, God loves you with an everlasting love. And that truth will set you free.[215] From death. From fear. From sin and guilt. From wicked desires and evil pleasures, envy and hate, and more.

Let God's love heal you

God's beloved, his people Israel, had sinned horribly and, in fulfillment of Hosea's prophetic message, would soon suffer terribly as a result. Their lands and homes would be taken from them, and they would be carried off into captivity. They would face far more anguish and affliction than they had ever known. God told them repeatedly what they could expect, as he does again in the last verses of chapter 13:

> "You may feel just fine right now,
>   but the wind of Yahweh is blowing in from the desert.
> It will parch your lands
>   and plunder your treasury.
> You will have no one to blame but yourselves,
>   because you rebelled against the One who loved you;

you will fall by the sword,

and your women and children will suffer horribly."[216]

But the tender, patient heart of God was not done with them. Even after his people ignored so many prophetic messages sent through Hosea, God wasn't done pleading with them:

O my Israel, come back to Yahweh, your God.

Your sins have cost you enough.

Cry out to him from your heart.

Come running back as fast as you can.

Say,

"Remove our sin;

receive us again,

and we will fulfill all we have promised you in the past.

We will not look to others to save us;

we will not trust in ourselves;

and we will no longer exalt the work of our hands

to the place of an idol.

You show mercy to the bereft;

show mercy to us."

"I will heal their wickedness;

I will lavish my love on them,

I will no longer be angry with them.

I will come to them like the dew to the grass;

I will make them my garden.

They will send down roots like the trees of Lebanon;

they will spread like aspens on the hillside.

They will thrive like a beautiful olive tree,

and spread their fragrance like a grove of cedars.

Many will gather in their luscious shade;
  they will spring up like a field of grain
and blossom like a vineyard of grapes.
  Their fame will spread far and wide."[217]

In spite of all that had happened and would happen in the years to come, God says, unequivocally, "I will heal." He promises that his people will yet experience wholeness, health, vitality, strength, beauty, and all manner of good, good things.

Let me tell you how that happens in my life. I have discovered that the only thing that will heal my waywardness, my unruly heart, my tendency to wander from God and get into all sorts of trouble, disappointment, and dysfunction is letting God love me. It's his love that heals me. That's why I pray. That's why I read the Bible every day. Because I have just one job every day, and that is to put myself in God's hands and let his love heal me and make me more and more like the tree he talks about in Hosea 14. That's my experience.

His love can heal you—physically, spiritually, emotionally. As Thomas Moore wrote in the original lines of his hymn, "Come Ye Disconsolate" (1816), "Earth has no sorrow that God cannot heal.". Let me suggest how it might happen for you. The Bible says,

> Is any one of you sick? He should call the elders of the church to pray over him and anoint him with oil in the name of the Lord. And the prayer offered in faith will make the sick person well; the Lord will raise him up. If he has sinned, he will be forgiven. Therefore confess your sins to each other and pray for each other so that you may be healed.[218]

Whether your sickness is a sickness of the heart, of the body, of the mind, memory, or soul, I want you to know that God's love can heal you—if you let it, if you place yourself in his arms, not just one time (such as when you "came forward" in a church service) but repeatedly, daily—letting his love wash over you, letting him lavish his love, letting him come to you like dew to the grass.

Let God's love empower you

In Hosea 14:8, God says to his people,

> "O my Israel, I will share nothing with idols.
>   I will be your one and only.
> I will be the one who fulfills your desires,
>   and you will want for nothing."[219]

The New International Version renders that last phrase,

> I am like a green pine tree;
>   your fruitfulness comes from me.[220]

In that verse, the next-to-last verse of the whole book of Hosea, God says to his people—to those he loves with a stubborn, unconditional, unrelenting love,

> "I am the vine; you are the branches. If a man remains in me and I in him, he will bear much fruit; apart from me you can do nothing."[221]

He is saying, "My child, I love you so much. Talk to me; I'll answer you. Lean on me; I'll care for you. Live in constant dependence on me; I'll *empower* you."

Hudson Taylor was an Englishman who loved God so much that when God called him to be a missionary to China, Taylor said yes and founded the China Inland Mission. Taylor's life was so empowered and used by God that when his son and daughter-in-law wrote his biography, they called it *Hudson Taylor's Spiritual Secret*.

And what was his spiritual secret?

> He knew that . . . the secret of overcoming lay in daily, hourly fellowship with God; and this, he found, could only be maintained by secret prayer and feeding upon the Word through which [God] reveals himself to the waiting soul.[222]

Taylor's biographers go on to quote Andrew Murray's exhortation:

> Take time. Give God time to reveal Himself to you. Give yourself time to be silent and quiet before Him, waiting to receive, through the Spirit, the assurance of His presence with you, His power working in you. Take time to read His Word as in His presence, that from it you may know what He asks of you and what He promises you. Let the Word create around you, create within you a holy atmosphere, a holy heavenly light, in which your soul will be refreshed and strengthened for the work of daily life.[223]

Imagine what it would be like to really live in the confident belief that our fruitfulness comes from God, that apart from him we can do nothing, that all our happiness, all our success, all our effectiveness, all the fruit of our efforts came not from our own cleverness, strength, good intentions, hard work, or good looks but from God, who loves us and will empower us if we but ask and trust and obey. Imagine if you took time, waiting on God, listening to him, talking to him, singing to him, reading his Word, basking in his loving presence. Then, maybe not all of a sudden, but day by day, week by week, month after month, the Spirit of God would begin to take more and more control

and you would experience more and more power

and fall more and more in love with him

and receive more and more answers from him

and become more and more aware of his care

until he became like a green pine tree to you, and you became more and more fruitful.

I pray that for you. I pray that for me. I pray that for the churches of Jesus Christ all over this world, that we will let God's love deliver us, heal us, and empower us, moment by moment, and for the rest of our earthly lives.

------------------------ § ------------------------

Lord God, make it so in my life. I cry out to you from my heart: remove my sin, receive me again, and I will fulfill all my heartfelt promises of the past. I will not look to others to save me. I will not trust in myself. I will not exalt the work of my hands to the place of an idol. You show mercy to the bereft; show mercy to me.

Heal my wickedness, thoroughly and finally. Lavish your love on me. Come to me like the dew on the grass. Make me your garden. Let me send down roots like the trees of Lebanon. Let me grow like aspens on the hillside. Cause me to thrive like a beautiful olive tree and spread my fragrance like a grove of cedars, that many will be blessed by me and that my fruit and influence may spread far and wide.

You, Lord, are my one and only. You are the one who fulfills my desires. I want for nothing. In Jesus' name, amen.

12

Telling the
Story of Love

*C*hester A. Arthur *was vice* president of the United States when President James A. Garfield was shot by a delusional former office seeker on July 2, 1881. In the weeks following the shooting, as the president languished between life and death, Arthur began to receive letters from a young woman he had never met. Her name was Julia Sand, and she was a thirty-two-year-old invalid.

Uninvited, she wrote to Arthur regularly during the two and a half months that Garfield's life hung in the balance. In one letter, she wrote,

> Your kindest opponents say: "Arthur will try to
> do right"—adding gloomily—"He won't succeed,
> though—making a man a President cannot change
> him." But making a man a President can change
> him! Great emergencies awaken generous traits which have
> lain dormant half a life. If there is a spark of true
> nobility in you, now is the occasion to let it shine.

Faith in your better nature forces me to write to you—
but not to beg you to resign. Do what is more difficult
& more brave. Reform![224]

Arthur, who had previously earned a reputation as an ineffectual politician and puppet of the powerful New York senator Roscoe Conkling not only read and saved Miss Sand's letters, he heeded them. Partly guided by her encouragement, Arthur surprised nearly everyone by advancing Garfield's agenda and instituting a number of effective reforms, prompting the journalist Alexander McClure to write, "No man ever entered the Presidency so profoundly and widely distrusted as Chester Alan Arthur, and no one ever retired ... more generally respected, alike by political friend and foe."[225]

Inspiration often comes from unexpected places. Often it arises from the shared experience and encouragement of others—even of people we don't know personally. For that reason, I chose to conclude this book with seven brief stories of people who have fallen in love with God. Each of them is personally known to me. They are my friends. And I have seen in each of them a passionate love for God that I hope will instruct and inspire you.

Because You Loved Me

Julie Webb's first glimpses of God came in a very traditional, liturgical church. "I experienced his presence many times in church," she says, "and worked very hard to please him, always trying to stay in a 'state of grace.'"

Then, some friends started inviting her to a Bible study not just once but repeatedly. She eventually gave in and began to learn that all her efforts counted for nothing:

Through that study, I discovered that grace is unmerited favor from God based on the sacrifice of Jesus Christ. I realized that Jesus didn't need my help—he simply wanted *me*. That was so liberating for me! I had been trying to earn my own salvation for years, and suddenly, there it was—given to me fully and freely, as an outright gift.

From that moment on, I was hungry for God's Word and all his promises. The Bible came alive for me. At one time, I was attending three Bible studies a week. I couldn't seem to get enough of his Word.

His love drew me to him. His grace set me free. His Word has been my comfort and support. His presence is my daily reality.

My Father's Eyes

Even in high school, Chris Russell was intent on following Jesus. Upon graduation, he enrolled in a Christian college. At the time, however, he was consumed with careful attention to what he saw (and the school enforced) as the "dos and don'ts" of the Christian life. He says, "I became an 'expert' at adding dos to my list and eliminating the don'ts." But there was little love in the equation.

Then, in his senior year, he got to know a married student who apparently picked up on his legalistic tendencies:

> He said, "Chris, you know I love my wife with all my heart. That love is the thing that makes me absolutely, completely committed and faithful to her. I would never want to do anything that would hurt my relationship with her. When we wake up in the morning, she does

not have to say, 'Now, Kevin, don't go out and commit adultery today, please.' My faithfulness to her stems out of my love and devotion to her, not from some list she gives me each morning."

Message received.

That day was a major turning point in my life. But I still don't think I truly fell in love with God until, some years later, I heard six words that changed everything: "We are going to have a baby!" I immediately began to feel a strong sense of love for my baby—who had not yet been born. That love only grew until the day my son, Quentin, was born. I found myself absolutely overwhelmed with love for this selfish, dependent, inarticulate bundle of humanity. I loved him more than words could express. I loved him absolutely and unconditionally. And I knew I would love him forever.

Suddenly, a spark ignited in my heart. Could this be how God loves me? This much? It was unfathomable to me. I had never connected with the Scriptures that say God loves us as a father loves his children. I grew up in a severely dysfunctional home. My father was harsh and abusive to me all throughout my childhood, and he left many scars on my heart. As a son, I couldn't identify with the Father's love. Once I became a father, however, I "got it." And when I identified with his love for me, it ignited *my* love for *him*. This was love: not that I love God, but that he loves me.[226]

"Behold what manner of love the Father has bestowed on us, that we should be called children of God!"[227]

Maybe I'm Amazed

Laurel Morgan says she first began to fall in love with God as a teenager attending a Christian summer sports camp. Time and experience only increased her love for God as she learned more about him and experienced more of life with him.

One such experience involved the movie *The Passion*—which depicted the final hours of Jesus' earthly life, when he was arrested, tried, and crucified. She had long been aware that Jesus died on the cross as a sacrifice for her sins. But the film drove it home to her in a way she had never before experienced:

> I was a college student, and during that film, I really came face to face with the depth of God's love for me. I could hardly believe how much of a sacrifice Jesus made for me. How could he do that for me? I am so undeserving of his sacrificial love. I remember saying as I left the theatre with tears in my eyes, "I am *so* in *love* with Jesus!" That representation of Jesus' trial and crucifixion helped me to see even more clearly that God alone is beyond worthy of all of our praise and love. It planted in me a deep, yearning desire to tell others about his love. I don't want a single drop of his blood to be wasted!
>
> Since then, I have continued to fall more and more in love with the Lord as I step out to know him, love him, and serve him with my life, and am met by his presence, strength, and encouragement every step of the way, in the ups *and* downs of life.

In the Still of the Night

Shortly after returning from teaching at a writers' conference, Virelle Kidder was in a deep sleep when she sensed God talking to her, nudging her awake in the middle of the night.

She was sure she heard him call her name. Then he said, "I thought you'd like to know how you really got your name, because you were wrong, you know."

"My name, Lord? But I know how I got my name. My mother told me, and she wouldn't lie." She had just offered her standard explanation of her name to a group of friends at the conference. She'd been spelling and explaining her name to people all her life, explaining that it was a combination of her parents' names: Virginia and Russell. When she was twelve, her mother added an "e" because everyone pronounced her name, "virile," something that never failed to make people laugh. "I never thought it funny at all," she says.

But now God was saying something different. "That may be what your parents thought, Virelle, but actually I named you. I just told them what I wanted."

"You named me, Lord?"

"Yes, I named you because I love you. I've always loved you. Since before you were born, you've been mine."

Lying in bed, as tears rolled onto her pillow, Virelle heard God inserting her name into his Word: "I've loved you with an everlasting love, Virelle. I formed you in your mother's womb. I know every hair on your head, planned every day in your life. I saw your tears as a child and saved them in a bottle. I have betrothed you to me forever. You are my bride, my beautiful one. There is no flaw in you. I loved you so much, I gave my Son to redeem you." And more.

"Until that night," she says, "nearly thirty years after receiving Christ as my Savior, I'd always known God loved me as he loved all his children, and I was the least of them. But that night—and ever since—I felt so loved by God, so permanently loved and fully redeemed, so chosen and cherished. He has always had my heart, but now he has every molecule in my body, every breath, every moment. His love drives my life, every single day."

Not Alone Anymore

Dewey Hughes says he felt alone, unloved, and uncared for in his early childhood. His father died when Dewey was two years old. His mother lived with several different men after that, and for some time, Dewey was passed from one family member to another. When he was seven years old, a family adopted him. A year later, Dewey says, the family took him back to his mother, explaining that "they didn't like me and didn't see how it could work."

A few months later, a family named Hughes adopted him. "In Mr. Hughes, I found unconditional love. Finally, I had a lap to crawl up into and feel safe and protected and loved. Within a few days, I was calling him 'Dad.' Why? Because he loved me, and made me feel safe. I grew to love him because he loved me. What I needed at that time, my dad gave me."

That, he says, is what he found in God through Jesus. "God gave me an unconditional love, a place of safety, a salvation, a peace, and a life in his Kingdom. I grew more and more in love with God because of what he added to me. Each day, I discover more that he adds to me and I grow a little more in love. I discover more holes and empty places in my life that only he can fill. How can you not love someone who completes you and constantly surrounds you with love, safety, and security?"

Unbreak My Heart

"I was a mess as a teenager," says Debbie Stacy. "My biological father walked out of my life when I was just a toddler. My mom then married a man whose only methods of discipline were to beat me with a studded belt and ground me for months at a time. I thought it couldn't get worse. Then it did.

"My next stepfather sexually abused me and took advantage of me in other ways, on many occasions. Going to church became a huge relief from my home life, a safe place where I would not be beaten or abused, but would actually be loved."

Then, one day, Debbie attended a regional church meeting with others from her denomination:

> I don't remember what the preacher was speaking about; I only remember how heavy my heart was as I sat in the chapel about three-fourths of the way to the back. As the invitation was given, tears began to flow down my cheeks; and before long I was sobbing, overwhelmed by the love of God. *How could someone love me so much?*
>
> My pastors approached me and asked if I wanted to go forward to pray, and they walked with me to the altar at the front. As I knelt there, I felt the fear, pain, abuse, and heaviness begin to lift from my heart. I understood that God loved me more than anyone had ever loved me—more than anyone could.
>
> I was a new person from that point on. But God had still more in store for me. Several years later, I was worshiping at a conference, when suddenly I felt as if I'd been hit in the head with a paper cup. I know it sounds odd. I thought so, too. But as I opened my eyes and

looked around, there was no sign of a paper cup, so I shrugged it off and continued to worship. Seconds later, I felt the Holy Spirit sweep into that room and envelop me and everyone around me. A lady behind me fell over onto the chairs in her row. Tears began to flow, and I experienced an overwhelming sensation of cleansing, healing, powerful love.

God continues to flood my soul with his love. He reminds me of his faithfulness. He draws me to himself, drives me to my knees, showers me with blessings, and lovingly corrects me when I need it—all of which creates a hunger in me to experience more and more of who he is and what he has for me. "O what a love between my Lord and I; I keep falling in love with Him over and over and over and over again."[228]

You Are So Beautiful

To Kasey Hitt, who was raised in a churchgoing and praying family, God was always like a family member who had consistantly been in her life. She remembers at the age of six "lying on my back in the grassy vacant lot next to our house looking up at the sky, and at other times lying on a tree branch in my front yard looking down at the ground. I was not particularly conscious of God in those moments, but I was able to rest and enjoy in his creation. Those times in nature brought and still bring a sense of peace, wholeness, completeness—*shalom*."

It was much later, however, during her teenage years, through passionate youth leaders and an active youth ministry, that she says she was invited to engage God on a public, social, and visible level:

I wholeheartedly did, and proclaimed it with my words, time ... and T-shirts. (Although I may also have become a little annoying in my adolescent zeal!)

Over the years, there have been spiritual highs ... along with dryness, burnout, and disappointment with life and with God. Still, through college, full-time youth ministry, marriage, seminary, a spiritual direction practice, and motherhood (as well as continuing to be a daughter, sister, and friend), I have experienced God *with, for,* and *in* me. Though at times this has brought joy and peace, I must admit that at other times, I've thought of giving up on the relationship altogether out of frustration.

However, this has allowed another spiritual practice to develop—recalling and pondering Peter's wonderful response after Jesus asked the Twelve if they wanted to leave him as others had done. "To whom shall we go?" Peter answered.[229] When I rage and cry—or even when I am numb—it doesn't take me long to arrive at the same place. Where would I go? Who else, what else, can provide the kindness and strength, the acceptance, hope, healing, and wholeness that I crave?

At such times, she says, something simple usually happens that reignites her awareness of God's love. "One of my children offers me a hug, a message from a friend comes, my husband's eyes fill with compassion, a gentle breeze rustles the leaves, a sunbeam falls on my face with such tenderness. In that vulnerable moment, I can almost hear God audibly say, *'I love you.'* And my tears echo my response."

The Power of Love

Doug Webb was raised in an abusive home with three older sisters and two brothers. By the time he was fourteen years old, he had endured many beatings and taken many risks. He was also an angry young man. "I would never walk away from a fight," he says, "and wouldn't hesitate to punch someone out for saying the wrong thing to me—or even looking at me the wrong way."

Unsurprisingly, at age sixteen, he was placed in a detention home for grand theft auto. "There was not a lot to do there," he says, "other than fight." So he did. His frequent fights landed him in a sparsely furnished room with no comforts . . . except a Gideon's Bible.

"I picked it up one day, and started reading. I will never forget my first reading. It was about King David, a little man with a mighty punch. I kept reading until the day my mother and my aunt came to take me home."

God had never been mentioned in his home as he was growing up. But then the youngest of his three older sisters married a Christian man. She began trying to persuade Doug to go to church, which he resisted. Finally, one Sunday night, "just to shut her up," he went to church with his sister and her husband. He survived, and agreed to go back a week later on a Wednesday night.

> Man, can I remember that night. The sermon that night was about David and how God forgave him for the wrong things he had done—which I know was no coincidence. For the first time in my life, I began to experience what it is like to be loved. Instead of being beaten into submission, God was drawing me with pure love, something I had never known or felt before. I stumbled

forward and knelt at the altar for more than an hour, crying uncontrollably. When I arose, I was a new person. I had a new heart. I no longer felt hate and contempt for anyone; I was simply overwhelmed with *love*.

That was only the beginning of my journey. In the many years since then, God has repeatedly overwhelmed me with his love, and I keep falling deeper in love with him. I talk to him daily, sometimes hourly, even minute by minute, and I fall deeper in love with him. I read his Word and I fall deeper in love with him. Everything I look at now—trees, flowers, water running in a creek, or a friendly smile—makes me fall deeper in love with him.

How different might my life have been, if not for God? Where would my temper have taken me? Where would I have ended up? I don't know. But I know this: Father God gave to *me*—someone it once seemed no one loved or could love—the ability to be loved and to fall in love with him, beyond all words and understanding.

Will You Still Love Me Tomorrow?

Darryl Handy says he fell in love with God because God fell in love with him first. But Darryl says,

> I still went a long time without knowing the depths of God's love for me. I knew and believed in Jesus. I was even pursuing Christ daily and serving in vocational ministry. But a few years ago, I lost my community and many comforts when I lost my job.
>
> It was a nightmare. I lost more than the job itself. I also lost opportunities. I lost friends. I lost my reputation.

But I didn't lose God. Far from it, in fact. God used this lack of stability in my life to show me the true stability I have in Christ. He showed me that, in Christ, I will never lose my place in him. He helped me see that he did not just deal with the needs I will have on Judgment Day; he deals with my frailty and shortcomings and brokenness every day.

And he didn't do that because of anything I have to offer. The Bible says, "God shows his love for us in that while we were still sinners, Christ died for us."[230] In other words, God's love for me didn't start when I finally got my act together—I never did and never will! His love is not dependent on me having my act together. God never said, "I'll love you if you do *such and such*;" he said, "I love you because of who I am"—and that's not ever going to change, because God never changes. And that changes everything for me. It means I don't have to live for success or human approval. I don't have to live in confusion or fear, wondering if God is pleased with me. In Christ, God *is* pleased with me. That is love. That is grace. That is amazing!

Why do I love God so much? I love God so much because God *has* loved, *does* love, and *will* love me ridiculously; not in ignorance of my weaknesses and sin, but despite my weaknesses and sin. And he keeps on showing his love and mercy for me every day as the Holy Spirit lives in me and God regards me with the love he has for Christ.[231] Who could not love a God like that?

Can't Help Falling in Love with You

Dawn Owens heard a speaker at a conference refer to God as a "gentleman." The phrasing was new to her. It brought her up short:

> I'd never heard it put that way before—as a gentleman who knocks on hearts' doors. A gentleman. To be honest, most of the men I knew were not gentlemen. Not even close. So I thought, *Why not give God a try?* If he could love me and treat me so kindly despite my sin, I wanted to get to know him. I decided to open that door.
>
> Days after that, I started reading the Bible, something I had never done before. The more I read, the more I wanted to read. The more time I spent learning, the more I wanted to learn. I couldn't seem to get enough. I'd wake early to pray and read my Bible and journal. My journaling was all about him, the things I was learning from him, the things I was learning about myself, and why I was falling in love with him. I'd break for lunch and, instead of eating with friends or coworkers, I'd sit in my office and read a Christian book or dig deeper into my Bible. I could hardly tear myself away to head back to work. I couldn't get home fast enough to dig in some more. I loved spending time with him. I loved that he loved me. I loved that he was all mine, which made me want to be wholly his. I discovered that in his presence I could be me, because he loved me for me. Before I knew it, he had thoroughly won my heart, with his gentlemanly ways and his loving words.
>
> Today, there is a depth to our intimacy that has developed from years of seeking him. The challenges,

pain, and suffering I have experienced have given me a richer grasp of his love for me. I say with the psalmist, "I love you, O LORD, my strength. The LORD is my rock and my fortress and my deliverer, my God, my rock, in whom I take refuge."[232]

All the Things You Are

I will let my story round off these personal accounts of falling in love with God. There is nothing spectacular to it. Having been raised in a devoted Christian family, I cannot remember a time when I didn't know God—though, as I've shared, I do remember my first conscious act of repentance and trust in him. My childhood was happy, if a little lonely.

Then, when I was fourteen years old, my mother was hospitalized after a yearlong struggle with breast cancer. I'm told I was a "mama's boy." I don't dispute it. My two older brothers had grown up and moved on, and, as the baby of the family, I had had her and my father all to myself. I needed that, as we had moved the year before from the only home I had ever known to a new city, a new neighborhood, a new school, and a new church. I had family in the area, but only one or two friends, and most weeks passed without seeing any of them.

At some point, someone must have told me—my father, perhaps—that my mother would not be coming home from the hospital. I think I had already known that but of course didn't want to face it. I couldn't imagine a world without my mother. I couldn't imagine my family without her. I couldn't imagine me without her. I never prayed more in my life. I never prayed more fervently. I never prayed with such faith and determination as when I prayed for her to healed.

She died that fall. I was devastated, of course, and had nowhere to go with my grief. My father and other family members were grieving as much as I was, and I probably closed myself off from those who offered comfort. I had only one refuge. Only one. I don't think I knew the hymn at the time, but Charles Wesley's "Jesus, Lover of My Soul" could have been my theme song:

> Other refuge have I none, hangs my helpless soul on Thee;
> Leave, ah! leave me not alone, still support and
>   comfort me.
> All my trust on Thee is stayed, all my help from Thee
>   I bring;
> Cover my defenseless head with the shadow of Thy wing.[233]

I went to God because I had nowhere else to go. I clung to him when I had nothing else to hold on to. I cried out to him though I had no idea what I was saying. And though my grief was deep and long, he held me throughout that long, dark night. He was my comforter, my refuge.

In the many (too many) years since then, he has not let me go, and I love him for that. He has been inexpressibly patient, loving, generous, and wise in all his dealings toward me.

I am in love with him because he forgave me and saved me when I was still a child. I am in love with him because his glories are infinite, his beauties are incalculable, and his attractions are unceasing. I am in love with him because he has always loved me—and I find that utterly baffling and gratifying all at the same time. I am in love with him because he was there for me when I needed him most (and not just once but many times over). I am in love with him because I can tell him anything and he won't dismiss or ridicule me. I am in love with him because he has not given up on me, though I have given him countless reasons to do so. I am in love with him because he has seen me at my worst and still puts up with me. I am in love with him because he remains faithful to me, through thick and thin. I am in love with him because he not only accepted my heart so many years ago—he pledged *his* to me. I am in love with him because he has always been true to that pledge. I am in love with him because he encourages, strengthens, shelters, heals, teaches, comforts, challenges, and provides for me. I am in love with him for those reasons, and many more.

I am in love with him because he has always fulfilled his Word in my life, as the last verse of Hosea puts it:

> Whoever is wise, pay attention;
>   whoever wants to prosper, listen up:
> God's ways are the only way to live.
>   Those who walk in them will be rewarded,
>   and those who stray from them will be sorry.[234]

Appendix

Author's Paraphrase
of the Book of Hosea

Hosea 1

¹The word of Yahweh came to a man named Hosea, the son of Beeri, back during the reigns of Uzziah, Jotham, Ahaz, and Hezekiah in Judah, and during the reign of Jeroboam the son of Joash in Israel.

²When Yahweh first began speaking through Hosea, he told him, "I want you to go and marry a whore. Have children with her, to demonstrate what my people have done by forsaking Yahweh." ³So Hosea did just that. He went and found Gomer, the daughter of Diblaim. He married her, and she got pregnant by him and gave birth to a son.

⁴When the boy was born, Yahweh told Hosea, "Name him Jezreel [meaning 'God will scatter'], for I will soon punish King Jehu and his royal house for the blood he shed in Jezreel, and I will abolish the kingdom of Israel. ⁵I will break Israel's military power in the Valley of Jezreel."

⁶Sometime later, Gomer got pregnant again and gave birth to a daughter. And Yahweh told Hosea, "Name her Lo-ruhamah [meaning 'Unloved'], for I am through showing love to Israel, I am done forgiving them. ⁷I will show love to Judah, and deliver them

from their enemies—but I'll make it clear that neither firepower nor strategy has saved them, but only Yahweh, their God."

[8]When Gomer had weaned Unloved, she became pregnant again and had another child, a son. [9]And Yahweh said, "Give him the name, Lo-ammi [meaning 'Not Mine'], because Israel is not my people, and I am not your God."

[10]Still, there will come a day when the people of Israel will be as numerous as sands on the seashore. In the very place where they were named "Not Mine" they will be called "God's Own." [11]And the people of Judah and of Israel will be reunited, as one, under One. What a day of rejoicing that will be, a day of exaltation, the day of Jezreel,

Hosea 2

[1]when you tell your brothers, "You are my flesh and blood," and say to your sisters, "You have been shown mercy."

> [2]"Persuade your mother, beg her—
>   for she is no wife to me,
>   and I am no longer her husband—
> That she stop whoring around,
>   and wipe away her adulterous makeup and perfume;
> [3]Or I will strip her myself,
>   naked as the day she was born,
>   remove all her pretenses
>   and expose her to utter desolation and emptiness.
> [4]And I won't stop there. I will show no mercy to
>   her children,
>   because they are the children
>   of her whorish behavior.

⁵She has brought shame on them,
>   running after her lovers
>   for the ease and the comforts they provide,
>   bread and water,
>   wool and flax, oil, and drink.
⁶So I will block her way with a thorny hedgerow.
>   I will wall her off from her wayward paths,
⁷so that when she heads out for a rendezvous,
>   she will fail
>   and won't even be able to find her lovers.
Then she will have to return to her husband,
>   to a time when things were better for her.
⁸She doesn't even know
>   that all along I was the one
>   giving her grain, wine, and oil.
I was the one who made sure she was taken care of,
>   while she would just spend my gifts on others.

⁹"So now I will take back my grain when it's ripe,
>   and my wine when it's ready.
I will repossess my wool and my flax,
>   which were intended to cover her with warmth
>   and respectability.
¹⁰Now, instead, I will expose her
>   while all her so-called lovers look on,
>   and no one will claim her from me.
¹¹I will shut down all her partying,
>   her feasts, and dances, and holidays.
¹²And I will level her gardens and orchards,
>   which she claimed as her right,

and counted as payment from her lovers.
I will turn them back into wilderness,
    fit only for wild animals.
[13]I will punish her for all her festivals to Baal,
    when she offered sacrifices to her idols
and bedecked herself with makeup and jewels for her
        lovers
    and forgot me,"
    says Yahweh.

[14]"But I will woo her again.
    I will take her out into the wilderness,
    and romance her with words.
[15]I will give her back her vineyards
    and turn her Valley of Trouble into a Doorway
        of Hope.
And she will respond to me as she did when she
    was young,
    when I brought her out of slavery in Egypt.

[16]"And then, Israel," Yahweh says,
    "you will call me 'my husband'
    instead of just 'my master.'
[17]I will make her forget the Baals;
    I will make their names foreign to her lips.
[18]And on that day I will make a peace treaty
    with the wild animals and birds,
    the rodents and reptiles,
and abolish the weapons of war from the land,
    so you can lie down in perfect peace and safety.
[19]And I will bind you to me forever

with bands of righteousness and justice,
of unwavering love and mercy.
²⁰I will be your faithful husband,
and you will truly know me.

²¹"And then I will answer,"
Yahweh says,
"and speak to the heavens,
and they will grant the earth's requests for rain,
²²and the earth will hear the thirsty cries of grain,
wine, and oil,
and restore plenty to Jezreel.
²³I will shower my love on Unloved,
and I will say to Not Mine,
'You are mine.' And he will answer me,
'You are my God.'"

Hosea 3

¹And Yahweh said to me, "Go and find your wife again, though she has betrayed you and taken up with another man. Love her as I love Israel, though they have prostituted themselves with other gods."

²So I scraped together the slave price—though it was all I had—and bought her. ³I told her, "You will live with me from now on. You will no longer be a whore. You will give yourself to no other man. And I will pledge the same to you."

⁴For my beloved, Israel, will be taken from me, and they will live many years in exile, in poverty, in emptiness. ⁵But they will return. They will long for me, and they will know what they lost. And they will be relieved and happy when I come to take them back.

Hosea 4

[1]Hear me now, my people, Israel,
>   for Yahweh has a grievance against you.
"There is no faithfulness or love in you;
>   you don't even know your own husband;
[2]You break promises, you lie, kill,
>   steal, and commit adultery.
You have no limits.
>   You go from bad to worse.
[3]That is why you're unhappy
>   and filled with anguish and regret.
Even the beasts of the field are languishing,
>   and the birds are depressed.
>   Not even the fish in the sea are thriving.

[4]"And you priests can argue all you want,
>   and try to blame someone else,
>   but you are at fault more than anyone;
[5]You're nothing but wayward children.
And you prophets are playing 'follow the leader'
>   in disobedience,
>   oblivious to the destruction of your mother, Israel.
[6]My beloved is ruined by her cluelessness!

"You priests reject knowledge,
>   so I reject you as priests.
You prophets have forgotten the Law,
>   I also will forget you.
[7]The more priests there are, the more sin there is.
>   The more pride, the more shame.

[8]The more sins the people commit, the more sacrifices
      they offer.
    The more sacrifices, the more the priests like it.
[9]Therefore, you are all in it together.
    As go the priests, so go the people.
    All will suffer the consequences of their actions.

[10]"You will gorge yourselves, but never be full;
    you will whore around, but gain nothing,
[11]because you have forsaken your Husband
    for idolatry and drunkenness,
    which make you stupid.
[12]My beloved would rather talk to a statue,
    and listen to a stick of wood.
For she has been seduced by a spirit of whoredom,
    and has left me in order to play the whore.
[13]Instead of worshiping me,
    my people sacrifice to idols on the mountaintops
    and give offerings on the hills;
they prostitute themselves in the shade
    of oak, poplar, and terebinth.
There, unsurprisingly, your daughters imitate your lewd
      behavior
    and your wives commit adultery.

[14]"But who can blame them
    when their priests and prophets,
    their fathers and husbands,
    have led the way into depravity, ignorance, and ruin?

¹⁵"How pathetic you've become, O Israel.
    Look at her and be warned, Judah.

"Stay away from the sacred circles.
    Steer clear of the house of idols.
    Don't deceive yourself into thinking
    you can mix the worship of Yawheh and idols.
¹⁶Israel is a stubborn mule;
    can I feed her like a lamb in verdant pastures?
¹⁷She clings to idols;
    let her be.
¹⁸They drink themselves silly,
    then they sin themselves stupid.
And those who should be correcting them
    love their shameful behavior.
¹⁹They are caught up in a whirlwind
    that will end only in shame.

Hosea 5

¹"Hear me now, you priests!
    Pay close attention, Israel!
Mark my words, royal family!
    I will put this as clearly as possible:
You have been an evil influence at Mizpah
    and led the people astray at Tabor.
²You have descended deep into sin, all of you,
    so I will go to great lengths to correct you.
³I know you intimately;
    I still see you clearly,
though you are covered in whoredom,
    you are defiled by your unfaithfulness.

⁴"You are ensnared in your own sin;

> your pride and stubbornness hold you back from
>> returning to me.

Your whoring ways have blinded you,

> so that you no longer even recognize my face.

⁵You are self-condemned;

> you are drunk with self-loathing,
>> dragging down Judah into the gutter with you.

⁶When you finally wake up

> and try to return to me,
> you won't know where to look;

I will be long gone.

⁷You have betrayed me,

> and borne the children of other lovers.

Now you and all you have will be consumed.

⁸"Sound the alarm now,

> for your destruction is coming:

⁹Certain,

> unavoidable,
> and extreme.

¹⁰Your leaders are crooked and corrupt,

> and I will no longer hold back the punishment
>> they deserve.

I will let loose on them.

¹¹I will cast you to the gutter

> since you were so determined to go there.

¹²I will chew you up like a moth,

> and will let your sins eat at you like dry rot.

¹³"When you, Israel, woke up to your own sickness,
> and Judah became aware of his condition,
you sent to Assyria for help,
> and appealed to that despot!
But he can't help you.
> He will only make matters worse.
¹⁴All my tenderness toward you has gotten me nowhere,
> so I will turn it off completely.
I will rip and shred you like a lion,
> I will tear you to pieces like a grizzly.
¹⁵Then I will return to my hiding place,
> until you have learned your lesson,
And come to your senses,
> and come looking for me," saying,

Hosea 6

¹"Come, let us return to Yahweh;
> for he has hurt us that he may heal us;
> he has wounded that he may make us whole.
²In short order, he will restore us;
> on the third day he will raise us up to a brand new
> life with him.
³Let us find him again; let us get to know him once more.
> Surely he will greet us like the dawn;
He will refresh us
> as he sends rain on the earth after a cold,
> hard winter."

⁴"What am I supposed to do with you, Israel?
> How can I get through to you, Judah?
Your love is like morning fog,

like dew that disappears at daybreak.
⁵Can you blame me for the harsh messages my
    prophets speak?
Can you really fail to be moved by my cutting words,
    my drastic actions?
⁶I want your faithful love, not your religious shows.
    I want you to want me, not just my favor.
⁷But like your first parents you have rejected me
    and walked out on me.
⁸You have turned places of refuge into crime scenes,
    and priests into robbers!
⁹Nothing is sacred to you;
    everything you touch becomes vile.
¹⁰I don't even recognize my beloved anymore;
    I see only a whore,
        only filth when I look at you.

¹¹"And you, Judah, are no better.

"Your fate will be no different."

Hosea 7

¹"Don't you see? I have wanted nothing but to love and
    heal Israel,
    but their sins have prevented me.
They cheat and lie,
    they steal and rob each other.
²They think I don't see them,
    or assume that I will look the other way.
But they pile up sin upon sin;
    how can I miss it?

³"Their evil behavior delights their king,
> and their officials laugh at their immorality.

⁴Every one of them is an adulterer;
> they are like ovens that never cool, even when empty.

⁵The king throws a party
> and the princes drink until they are sick
> and debase themselves with mockers.

⁶Their hearts are ovens of treachery;
> their hatred smolders through the night
> and blazes into flame with the morning.

⁷The fires of their rage consume their leaders;
> they drop like moths in a flame.
> None of them calls to me.

⁸"My people try to have it both ways;
> they are half baked.

⁹Godless people sap their strength,
> and they don't even see it;

they're growing old before their time,
> yet they don't see what they're doing to themselves.

¹⁰Their arrogance is so obvious,
> yet they are blinded by it;
> it prevents them from returning to Yahweh,
>> despite everything.

¹¹"My Israel is a silly bird,
> confused and fickle,
> flitting to Egypt for help, flying off to Assyria.

¹²I will toss my net
> and trap them like the flighty creatures they are.
> I will teach them, one way or the other.

[13]I will make them sorry for their waywardness.

  I will inflict pain on them!
I would have liked to be kind to them,

  but they won't stop lying to me.
[14]I would prefer for them to ask me for help,

  but they prefer to be miserable;
they cut themselves and appeal to idols,

  and turn away from me.
[15]I am the one who cared for them and trained them,

  but they act like I'm their enemy.
[16]They are willing to try anything;

  they will turn to anyone except me!
They are like a warped bow;

  they can't shoot straight to save their life!
Their leaders will get what they deserve,

  and those they've tried to impress will laugh at them.

Hosea 8

[1]"Get ready to sound the alarm!
The vultures are circling, ready to prey on my people,

  for they have rejected my love
  and rebelled against my law.
[2]They never hesitate to say,

  'God, help us out. Give us a hand!'
[3]But they have slapped away my hand once too often;

  now let their enemies go after them.
[4]They choose their own poison;

  installing kings without thought of me,
  crowning princes all on their own.

With silver and gold they make idols,
    fashioning their own destruction.
⁵I reject your golden calf, O Samaria.
    It incites my anger.
How long will you be so devoid of conscience?
⁶It is a toy! You made it yourself!
    How can you worship it as a god?

⁷"You know the crop is always greater than the seed;
    sow the wind, and you will reap a whirlwind.
The things you are doing are empty and useless;
    like wheat with no head, it will produce nothing.
What little it may yield will not be worth harvesting.
⁸Do you not see? Israel is being eaten alive;
    they're already known among the nations as
        has-beens.
⁹They are like a donkey in heat,
    trotting off to Assyria,
      looking for love.
¹⁰They have sold themselves to this lover and that lover,
    but that will soon end.
They will be dominated by one lover,
    and they won't like it.

¹¹"My beloved has built many altars,
    and made them places for sinning instead
      of cleansing.
¹²I gave them my beautiful laws for their own good,
    yet they treated them like an affliction.
¹³They still make sacrificial offerings,
    but with no regard for what I require.

I do not accept them.
Their sacrifices are useless; they accomplish nothing!
I will punish them.
I will send them back to Egypt.
[14]For they have utterly forgotten me.
and focused on building palaces and
fortresses instead.
So I will send fire on their cities,
and destruction on her fortifications."

Hosea 9

[1]Don't be so sure of yourself, Israel.
Don't act like you're as happy as everyone else,
sleeping around while forsaking your God.
You've sold yourself everywhere you can,
[2]but you're still hungry, aren't you?
There's not enough wine in the world to fill
your emptiness.
[3]You won't be around much longer.
You'll be a slave to Egypt again;
you'll be Assyria's whore.
[4]Soon you won't be able to worship the Lord if you
wanted to;
even if you try, your offerings will be unclean,
like moldy bread,
good for nothing and no one but yourself.

[5]What will your holidays and parties be like then?
[6]You may run, but you can't hide;
Egypt will find you,
and you'll be buried in the sands of Memphis.

Your silver will tarnish
    and your homes will crumble.
[7]You won't be able to postpone punishment any longer;
    you'll have to pay for your sins.
You'll know: the prophets aren't as dumb as you think,
    the true worshipers of Yahweh won't look so foolish
when you are called to account for your great sin
    and hatefulness.
[8]The prophet is God's watchman over Israel;
yet they are always trying to trap him,
    pouring out hatred on him.
[9]They have deeply corrupted themselves
    as in the days of Gibeah:
he will remember their iniquity;
    he will punish their sins.

[10]"Like one who finds grapes in the wilderness,
    I found Israel.
Like one who sees the first fruit on a fig tree
    I was delighted to see your fathers.
But they came to Baal-peor
    and bound themselves to a disgusting idol,
    and took on the stink of their vile partner.
[11]Israel's glory will flutter off like a bird—
    they will have no births to celebrate,
[12]and, worse,
    they will grieve the loss of their heirs.
They will be sorry
    that I have left them!

¹³I knew my Israel
  when they were like a young palm planted in a
    pleasant place,
  but they are leading their children to destruction."

¹⁴O LORD, I don't even know what to ask for such
    faithless people,
  except for wombs that won't give birth
  and breasts that won't give milk.

¹⁵"From the beginning of our relationship,
  they treated me wickedly.
They worked overtime
  to earn my hatred and rejection.
I will give them what they want
  and let them follow their rebellious leaders.
¹⁶My Israel is diseased;
  they are sick from the bottom of their hearts;
  there is no health in them.
Even if they manage to give birth,
  I will take their children away."

¹⁷My God will turn his back on them
  who turned their hearts from him;
  they will be nomads.

Hosea 10

¹Israel is a flourishing vine
  laden with fruit.
Yet the more they prosper,
  the more pagan altars they build.

The more prosperity,
    the more profligacy.
[2]Their hearts are fickle;
    and no amount of pleading can ease their guilt.
Yahweh will smash their altars
    and demolish their idols.

[3]When that happens, they will say,
    "We have no god, we have no king,
    who is there to help us?"
[4]They will say anything
    to get what they want.
They are quick to make promises,
    and quick to break them.
Disputes spring up among them
    like noxious weeds in a plowed field.
[5]They are so proud of their idols,
    and get so worked up when anything threatens them.
[6]But their idols will be boxed up and shipped off;
    their pride will become their shame.
[7]Those who led them in their idolatry will be swept away
    like a twig floating downstream.
[8]Their precious high places will be brought low.
    Weeds will grow up over their altars,
and they will try to hide themselves
    in their shame.

[9]"From the very first, you have betrayed me, O Israel;
    and you have only continued in the way you began.
    And so it will be until the end.
[10]So it will be until they receive what they deserve.

Foreign armies will crush them
for their repeated sin.
[11]My Israel was a tame calf that loved to serve her master,
and I treated her tenderly;
but no more.
I will put a yoke on her neck,
and she will bend low under it.
[12]Oh, my people, sow righteousness,
reap love and mercy.
Break up your fallow ground,
and seek Yahweh *now*,
that he may come and rain righteousness upon you.
[13]But you have scattered wickedness,
and so you have reaped ugliness;
you have gorged yourself on lies.
You have trusted only in yourself
and surrounded yourself with defenses.
[14]But it will do you no good.
Unimaginable destruction is coming your way,
utter devastation.
[15]It will be nothing you don't deserve,
nothing your evil hasn't invited.
When that day dawns,
all you have known will come to an end.

Hosea 11

[1]"When Israel was a child, I loved him.
I called them out of Egypt like a midwife coaxing an
infant from the womb.

²But the more lovingly I spoke to them,
    the farther they ran away;
they played with their Baals on the hills
    and burned offerings to idols.
³It was I who had taught them to walk;
    I cradled them in my arms,
        but they did not know that I was the one who kissed
            their boo-boos.
⁴I led them tenderly, with cords of kindness,
    as one guides a pet around a yard.
I loosened the harness so it wouldn't rub,
    and fed them by hand.

⁵"They will not return to slavery in Egypt
    but they will end up in bondage to Assyria
    rather than return to me.
⁶Violence rages in their cities,
    enemies devour them left and right
    because of their foolish plans,
⁷yet they are hell-bent on rejecting me.
    Now, if they were to call out to me,
    it would be no use.

⁸"How can I give you up, my Israel?
    How can I let you go?
How can I watch you be ruined?
    How can I endure your destruction?
My heart breaks;
    my compassion rekindles.
⁹How can I carry out my anger?
    I will not destroy my Israel;

for I am God and not a man,
    I am the Holy One in your midst,
    and I will not utterly destroy you.
[10]You will follow me again.
I will roar like a lion,
    and my children will come trembling from
        a distance;

[11]they will fly back to me like birds from Egypt,
    and like doves from Assyria,
and I will restore them to their homes, I promise.

[12]My Israel has encircled me
    with lies and pretense.
And Judah is out of control,
    repeatedly running away from my faithful love.

Hosea 12

[1]My Israel tries to gorge themselves on emptiness,
    and sucks wind all day;
they add falsehood to falsehood
    and multiply it with violence;
they treaty with Assyria,
    and trade with Egypt.

Yahweh's indictment of Israel and Judah
[2]Yahweh has filed charges against them.
    They will be punished;
    they will pay.

³Their ancestor fought with his brother in the womb,
    and wrestled with God in the night.
⁴He struggled, and won;
    he wept and found blessing.
He met God there,
    and God met him,
⁵Yahweh, the Almighty God,
    whose name is forever.
⁶Do likewise!
    Call on God! Struggle with him!
    Wrestle with love and justice,
    and don't give up.

⁷But you would rather continue your cheating ways.
⁸You tell yourself you are rich
    because no one has caught you yet.
⁹"I am Yahweh, the One who rescued you from Egypt;
    I will make you nomads again,
    as you were in the desert.
¹⁰I spoke to the prophets,
    and gave them visions and warnings,"

¹¹but it had no effect on you,
    on your idolatry
    and your sin.
¹²Your ancestor Jacob fled his home
    and slaved many years for his wife.
¹³But Yahweh brought Israel out of Egypt,
    and guarded her carefully through the years.
¹⁴But she has spit in his face;
    so Yahweh will let her suffer the consequences.

Hosea 13

¹There once was a time when the word of my people
      meant something;
  they were respected,
  but all that was lost through sin.
²And now there is no end to their sin.
  They manufacture idols,
  and craft them carefully,
  as if it matters what kind of cow an idolater kisses.
³They are now like the morning mist
  like the dew the sun chases away,
like chaff that is blown by the wind
  or smoke that fades into the atmosphere.

⁴"But I am Yahweh,
  the God who rescued you from Egypt;
I am the only true God,
  for there is no other savior besides me.
⁵I was the one who knew you in the desert,
  in those waterless tracts;
⁶yet when you filled your bellies,
  you puffed out your chest and forgot all about me.
⁷So I will be a lion to you;
  I will stalk you like a leopard.
⁸I will pounce on you like a an angry she-bear;
  I will rip and tear,
  and devour and destroy.

⁹"Who will help you then, my Israel?

Who will rescue you when I, who have been
      your helper,
    turn against you?
[10]Will your king save you?
    What about your nobles?
You asked for a king to rule you,
     [11]and I gave you what you wanted,
    until I took him away in my anger.
[12]Your accounts are coming due;
    payment will be required.
[13]You will be like a baby, reluctant to be born,
    who must be ripped from the womb.

[14]"However, I will yet ransom you from the grave.
    I will redeem you from Death.
    I will say, "Where is your power now, Death?
    Where is your sting, Grave?"

"And nothing will change my mind
[15]You may feel just fine right now,
    but the wind of Yahweh is blowing in from
        the desert.
It will parch your lands
    and plunder your treasury.
[16]You will have no one to blame but yourselves,
    because you rebelled against the One who loved you;
    you will fall by the sword,
    and your women and children will suffer horribly."

Hosea 14

[1]O my Israel, come back to Yahweh, your God.
    Your sins have cost you enough.
[2]Cry out to him from your heart.
    Come running back as fast as you can.
Say,
    "Remove our sin;
    receive us again,
    and we will fulfill all we have promised you in
        the past.
[3]We will not look to others to save us;
    we will not trust in ourselves;
and we will no longer exalt the work of our hands
    to the place of an idol.
You show mercy to the bereft;
    show mercy to us."

[4]"I will heal their wickedness;
    I will lavish my love on them,
    I will no longer be angry with them.
[5]I will come to them like the dew to the grass;
    I will make them my garden.
They will send down roots like the trees of Lebanon;
    [6]they will spread like aspens on the hillside.
They will thrive like a beautiful olive tree,
    and spread their fragrance like a grove of cedars.
[7]Many will gather in their luscious shade;
    they will spring up like a field of grain
and blossom like a vineyard of grapes.
    Their fame will spread far and wide.

⁸O my Israel, I will share nothing with idols.
    I will be your one and only.
I will be the one who fulfills your desires,
    and you will want for nothing."

⁹Whoever is wise, pay attention;
    whoever wants to prosper, listen up:
God's ways are the only way to live.
    Those who walk in them will be rewarded,
    and those who stray from them will be sorry.

Endnotes

1   Edan Ahbez, "Nature Boy," Warner/Chappell Music, 1947.

2   Genesis 2:21–25 NLT.

3   Genesis 2:19–20.

4   Genesis 2:24 NLT.

5   Genesis 2:25 NLT.

6   Genesis 1:26 ESV.

7   Gregory of Nyssa, "Dogmatic Treatises, etc." Christian Classics Ethereal Library, 3, http://www.ccel.org/ccel/schaff/npnf205.x.ii.ii.iv.html.

8   Genesis 2:7 KJV.

9   Deuteronomy 6:5 NCV.

10   Matthew 22:36–38 NLT.

11   1 Corinthians 6:17 NIV.

12   Ephesians 3:19.

13   Deuteronomy 7:7–8 NLT.

14   Deuteronomy 6:5 NCV.

15   Hosea 1:1, author's paraphrase.

16   2 Kings 17:1–7.

17   Zechariah 3:1–10.

18   Zechariah 3:9.

19   Hosea 1:1, author's paraphrase.

20   1 Samuel 15:10 NIV.

21   2 Samuel 7:4 NIV.

22   1 Kings 17:2 NIV.

23   Isaiah 38:4 NIV.

24   Jeremiah 32:26 NIV.

25   Ezekiel 1:3 NIV.

26   Jonah 1:1 NIV.

27   Hosea 1:1, author's paraphrase.

28   Samuel Logan Brengle, *The Soul-Winner's Secret* (London: Salvationist, 1903), 101, 104.

29   Hosea 1:2, author's paraphrase.

30   Hosea 1:3, author's paraphrase.

31   Yvonne Lehman, *In Shady Groves* (Grand Rapids, MI: Chosen Books, 1983).

32   Hosea 1:3b–5, author's paraphrase.

33   D. Stuart Briscoe, *Taking God Seriously* (Waco, TX: Word Books, 1986), 16.

34   Hosea 1:6–9, author's paraphrase.

35   Hosea 1:3b, author's paraphrase.

36   Hosea 1:6a, author's paraphrase.

37   Hosea 1:8b, author's paraphrase.

38   John 8:10–11 NIV.

39   Romans 8:1 NIV.

40   Psalm 139:8a NIV.

41   1 Corinthians 6:9–11 NIV, emphasis mine.

42   John 15:16 NIV.

43   Ephesians 2:1, 3, 4–5 NIV.

44   Ephesians 3:18 NIV.

45   See John 13:4–5, 21–26.

46   (see John 13:31-38, 18:15-27, and 21:15-18).

47   John 21:7.

48   Hosea 1:10–2:1, author's paraphrase.

49   Briscoe, *Taking God Seriously*, 23.

50   Hosea 2:2–7, author's paraphrase.

51   Hosea 2:8–9, author's paraphrase.

52   Deuteronomy 8:11–14 NIV.

53   Hosea 2:9–13, author's paraphrase.

54   Hosea 2:14–23, author's paraphrase.

55   Hosea 2:2, author's paraphrase.

56   Hosea 2:5, author's paraphrase.

57   Joni Mitchell, "Big Yellow Taxi" (Warner Brothers, 1970).

58   Psalm 139:13.

59   Deuteronomy 8:18.

60   1 Samuel 2:7 NIV.

61   David McIntyre, *The Hidden Life of Prayer* (Plantation, FL: Fowler Digital Books, 2010), location 465–466.

62   James 1:17 NIV.

63   Hosea 2:8b.

64   Kim and Krickitt Carpenter, *The Vow: The True Events That Inspired the Movie* (Nashville: B&H, 2012), 82.

65   Hosea 2:14–15, author's paraphrase.

66   Francis Thompson, *The Hound of Heaven*, public domain.

67   Carpenter, *Vow*, 145.

68   Hosea 2:2–7, author's paraphrase.

69   Ben and Robin Pasley, "I Will Not Forget You," Corinthian Music, copyright 1999.

70   Brian Doerksen, "Light the Fire Again," Mercy/Vineyard, copyright 1994.

71   Charles Wesley, "I Have No Claim on Grace," public domain.

72   "Beautiful," lyrics and music by Linda Perry © 2001 Stuck in the Throat Music / Famous Music Corporation administered for the world (ex USA) by BMG Music Publishing International.

73   Romans 7:18 NIV.

74   Hosea 2:14, author's paraphrase.

75   Hosea 2:14b, author's paraphrase.

76   Hosea 2:15, author's paraphrase.

77   Ephesians 3:18–19 NIV.

78   Hosea 2:19–20 NIV.

79   Hosea 3:1, author's paraphrase.

80   Hosea 3:1–2, author's paraphrase.

81   This scenario seems to correspond to the descriptions in Hosea 2.

82   Hosea 3:2, author's paraphrase.

83   Hosea 3:2 ESV.

84   Exodus 21:32a NIV.

85   Hosea 3:3–5, author's paraphrase.

86   Hosea 3:4 *The Message*.

87   Hosea 3:1, author's paraphrase.

88   Romans 7:14b, 24–25 NIV.

89   Sidney Cox, "The Savior Sought and Found Me," copyright Salvation Army, 1953.

90   Matthew 26:14–16 *The Message.*

91   1 Peter 1:18–19 NIV.

92   Mark 10:45 and Matthew 20:28 NIV.

93   Hosea 3:3, author's paraphrase.

94   Hosea 3:3 CEB.

95   Hosea 3:4–5, author's paraphrase.

96   1 Peter 1:8 KJV.

97   Malachi 3:6 NIV.

98   James 1:17 NIV.

99   Hosea 4:1–6, author's paraphrase.

100   2 Corinthians 4:6 NIV.

101   Hosea 4:6a KJV.

102   Hosea 6:3 NLT, italics added.

103   Hosea 4:7–13, author's paraphrase.

104   St. Augustine, *The Confessions of St. Augustine,* translated by Edward B. Pusey, D.D. (New York: Collier Books, 1966), 11.

105   Annie Dillard, *Pilgrim at Tinker Creek* (New York: Harper's Magazine Press, 1974), 171.

106   Hosea 4:10–12a NIV.

107   Hosea 4:14–19, author's paraphrase.

108   Hosea 4:15b, author's paraphrase.

109   Deuteronomy 6:4 NIV.

110   Hosea 5:1–4, author's paraphrase.

111   Romans 3:10 NIV.

112   John 15:5 NIV.

113   Hosea 5:4a, author's paraphrase.

114   Hosea 5:4 NIV, italics added.

115   Hosea 5:8–11, author's paraphrase.

116   Hosea 5:8a ESV, emphasis mine.

117   Hosea 5:12–15, author's paraphrase.

118   Romans 11:22 KJV.

119   Jen Chaney, "Eddie Fisher: A singer best remembered for scandal," *The Washington Post*, September 24, 2010, http://voices.washingtonpost.com/celebritology/2010/09/eddie_fisher_a_singer_best_rem.html.

120   David Wigg, "My Husband Picked up the Phone and I Said 'I Know You're in Bed with Liz Taylor': Debbie Reynolds on the Pain of Losing Her Husband," *Daily Mail*, April 23, 2010, http://www.dailymail.co.uk/tvshowbiz/article-1268158/Debbie-Reynolds-losing-husband-Eddie-Fisher-Elizabeth-Taylor.html#ixzz1xtbtLQJJ.

121   Hosea 6:1–3, author's paraphrase.

122   Hosea 6:7–11, author's paraphrase.

123   1 Samuel 16:7 NLT.

124   Matthew 3:8; Luke 3:8 NIV.

125   Mark 7:6 NIV.

126   Hosea 6:4–6, author's paraphrase.

127   Deuteronomy 6:4–6 NIV.

128   http://www.sugardaddyforme.com.

129   Ibid.

130   Briscoe, *Taking God Seriously*, 21.

131   Howell Harris, quoted in David Martin Lloyd-Jones, *The Puritans* (Edinburgh: Banner of Truth, 1987), 300.

132   Hosea 7:1–7, author's paraphrase.

133   John Calvin, *Commentary on Hosea* (Grand Rapids, MI: Christian Classics Ethereal Library, 1999), http://www.ccel.org/ccel/calvin/calcom26.html.

134   Revelation 2:5b *The Message*.

135   Warren W. Wiersbe, *The Bible Exposition and Commentary: Wisdom and Poetry* (Colorado Springs: Cook Communications Ministries, 2003), 693.

136   Hosea 7:8–10, author's paraphrase.

137   Will J. Brand, "When From Sin's Dark Hold Thy Love Had Won Me," *The Song Book of The Salvation Army* (New York: Salvation Army, 1967), 135.

138   Hosea 7:11–15, author's paraphrase.

139   Jeremiah 2:13 ESV.

140   Luke 10:42.

141   Hosea 7:16, author's paraphrase.

142   Hosea 7:16b, *Moffatt*.

143   Revelation 2:5 NIV.

144   G. Campbell Morgan, *Voices of Twelve Hebrew Prophets* (Grand Rapids, MI: Baker Book House, 1975), 43.

145   1 Corinthians 13:4–7 NIV.

146   Hosea 8:1, author's paraphrase.

147   Compiled from Psalm 68.

148   Hosea 8:2–3, author's paraphrase.

149   Hosea 8:4–7, author's paraphrase.

150   1 Kings 12:26–29 NIV.

151   Hosea 8:8–14, author's paraphrase.

152   Hosea 9:1-7, author's paraphrase.

153   Jonathan Edwards, quoted in *Prayers for Today: A Yearlong Journey of Contemplative Prayer*, Kurt Bjorklund (Chicago: Moody, 2011), 51.

154   Hosea 9:8–9, author's paraphrase.

155   Proverbs 1:23–25 CEB.

156   Hosea 9:10–10:2a, author's paraphrase.

157   Morgan, *Voices of Twelve Hebrew Prophets*, 45.

158   Hosea 10:2b–4, author's paraphrase.

159   Romans 8:1, NCV.

160   Hosea 10:5–10, author's paraphrase.

161   Ed Stetzer, *Subversive Kingdom* (Nashville, TN: Broadman & Holman, 2012), 138.

162   John Calvin, *Institutes of the Christian Religion*, Ed. John T. McNeill (Philadelphia: Westminster, 1960), 1:108.

163   Hosea 10:11–15, author's paraphrase.

164   1 Timothy 1:15 KJV.

165 Charles Wesley, "Love Divine, All Loves Excelling."

166 Elizabeth Barrett Browning, *Sonnets from the Portuguese* (New York: Thomas Y. Crowell, 1936), 43.

167 Hosea 11:1–3, author's paraphrase.

168 Exodus 4:22–23 NIV (1984).

169 Psalm 139:13, 15–16 NIV.

170 Anne Lamott, *Operating Instructions: A Journal of My Son's First Year* (New York: Fawcett Columbine, 1993), 187.

171 Lamott, 214.

172 Hosea 11:4–7, author's paraphrase.

173 Hosea 10:11, author's paraphrase.

174 Dorothy Thrupp, "Savior, Like a Shepherd Lead Us."

175 Hosea 11:8–9, author's paraphrase.

176 Though not included in the author's paraphrase, the original language of verse 8 actually specifies Admah and Zeboiim, two of the cities God destroyed when he judged Sodom and Gomorrah.

177 Albert Orsborn, "He Cannot Forget Me," *The Song Book of The Salvation Army* (New York: Salvation Army, 1967), 320.

178 Hosea 11:10–11, author's paraphrase.

179 Hosea 11:4 NLT.

180 Hosea 11:12–12:2, author's paraphrase.

181 Robert Robinson, "Come, Thou Fount of Every Blessing."

182 Psalm 63:5 NIV.

183 1 Peter 2:3 NIV.

184 Hebrews 6:4 NIV.

185 Hebrews 6:5 NIV.

186 2 Kings 17:1–4.

187 Hosea 12:3–5, author's paraphrase.

188 Revelation 2:5a NIV.

189 Hosea 12:6, author's paraphrase.

190 Hosea 12:6 NLT.

191 Hosea 12:6 NCV.

192 Simon Tugwell, quoted in Brent Curtis and John Eldredge, *The Sacred Romance* (Nashville, TN: Thomas Nelson, 1997), 81.

193 Revelation 2:5 *The Message*.

194 Isaiah 55:7 NIV.

195 Genesis 32:22–31 NIV.

196 Genesis 32:25 CEV.

197 Hosea 12:6, author's paraphrase.

198 Hosea 12:6 NLT.

199 Psalm 34:8 NIV.

200 Psalm 63:5 NIV.

201 Genesis 32:26.

202 Proverbs 21:1.

203 Hosea 13:1–13, author's paraphrase.

204 Hosea 13:14, author's paraphrase.

205 Hosea 13:14a, author's paraphrase.

206 Mark 10:45 NIV.

207 Titus 3:3–7 NLT.

208 1 Corinthians 15:55–57 NIV.

209   C. S. Lewis, *The Screwtape Letters* (West Chicago, IL: Lord and King, 1976), 34.

210   I wrote about "How I Got My Groove Back" here: http://desperatepastor.blogspot.com/2010/07/how-i-got-my-groove-back.html.

211   Psalm 124:8, paraphrased.

212   Quoted in William Backus and Marie Chapian, *Telling Yourself the Truth* (Minneapolis, MN: Bethany House, 1980), 18.

213   Ephesians 2:10 NLT.

214   Philippians 4:13 NKJV.

215   John 8:32.

216   Hosea 13:15–16, author's paraphrase.

217   Hosea 14:1–7, author's paraphrase.

218   James 5:14–16a NIV.

219   Hosea 14:8, author's paraphrase.

220   Hosea 14:8b NIV.

221   John 15:5 NIV.

222   Dr. & Mrs. Howard Taylor, *Hudson Taylor's Spiritual Secret* (Chicago: Moody Press, 1987), 234–235.

223   Ibid., 235–236.

224   Candice Millard, *Destiny of the Republic: A Tale of Madness, Medicine and the Murder of a President* (New York: Anchor Books, 2011), 208.

225   Thomas C. Reeves, *Gentleman Boss: The Life of Chester A. Arthur* (New York: Alfred A. Knopf, 1975).

226   1 John 4:10 ESV.

227   1 John 3:1a NKJV.

228   Lanny Wolfe, "I Keep Falling in Love with Him," Lanny Wolfe Music, 1976 (Admin. by Gaither Copyright Management).

229   John 6:68, NIV.

230   Romans 5:8 ESV.

231   2 Corinthians 5:21.

232   Psalm 18:1–2 ESV.

233   Charles Wesley, "Jesus, Lover of My Soul."

234   Hosea 14:9, author's paraphrase.